City Managers in Legislative Politics

The Urban Governors Series

City Managers
in Legislative Politics

Ronald O. Loveridge
University of California, Riverside

The Bobbs-Merrill Company, Inc.   Indianapolis   New York

Heinz Eulau, Stanford University
Kenneth Prewitt, University of Chicago

Coeditors, The Urban Governors Series

To Marsha, Joan, and Kelly

Editors' Preface

This study, like the others in *The Urban Governors* series, is based on data collected by the City Council Research Project, Institute of Political Studies, Stanford University. The CCRP was a collaborative research and research-training program made possible by grants from the National Science Foundation. Members of the project, all at one time or another doctoral candidates in political science at Stanford, were Betty H. Zisk, Boston University; Ronald O. Loveridge, University of California; Robert Eyestone, University of Minnesota; Peter A. Lupsha, Yale University; Thomas E. Cronin, University of North Carolina; Gordon Black, University of Rochester; Katherine Hinckley, Rice University; Stephen Ziony, City University of New York; Charles F. Levine, University of Illinois at Chicago Circle; and Helmut Kramer, Institute for Advanced Studies, Vienna. Heinz Eulau, Stanford University, served as principal investigator and Kenneth Prewitt, University of Chicago, served as associate investigator.

Although the CCRP was centrally directed, each investigator contributed to the design of the research and was free to utilize the commonly collected data as he saw fit. Each monograph in this series, therefore, reflects the writer's own theoretical and substantive interests, and each writer is alone responsible for what he has written. Yet, the series as a whole constitutes more than the sum of its parts. At the heart of the project was a concern with decision-making in small, natural-state legislative groups. Decisions coming out of city councils have far-ranging consequences for the lives of residents in a metropolitan region. While the project's central focus was on legislative behavior within the city council, topics as diverse as problems of metropolitan integration or the socialization and recruitment experiences of individual councilmen became matters of inquiry. As a result, the individual monographs in this series are variously linked not only to the literature on legislatures and representation, but also to the literature on urban government, policy outputs, elections, interest group politics, and other aspects of political life.

The "web of government" is complex, and its complexity makes for complex analysis. We solved the problem of complexity in the real world of politics by dividing the analytic labor among the project's members, and it is for this reason that each volume in this series must stand on its own feet. But we would also insist that each volume contribute to the common enterprise of managing the intricacy of political life without imposing on it any fashionably simple model of what politics is all about. In general, the units of analysis used in the different monographs are individual councilmen. A comprehensive study based on councils rather than on councilmen as units of analysis is also in preparation.

The major source of data was interviews conducted with 435 city councilmen in eighty-seven cities of the greater San Francisco Bay region during 1966 and 1967. A description of the research site, research design, interview success, and related matters can be found in Appendix D. Some of the interviews were conducted by the members of the research team, but the bulk were undertaken by a group of professional interviewers including Jean J. Andrews, Sheryl Brown, Marion N. Fay, Helen M. Smelser, Sofia K. Thornburg, Mary E. Warren, and Betty E. Urquhart. Peter Lupsha served as field coordinator, Jean Stanislaw as research aide, and Virginia Anderson as project secretary. During the analytical phase of the project, we have had the help of Sally Ferejohn as research assistant, Tex Hull as computer adviser, and Lois Renner as secretary.

Heinz Eulau
Kenneth Prewitt

Acknowledgments

Acknowledgments are a traditional ritual in most books. To the uninitiated, this ritual seems perfunctory, dictated by the good manners of the men of letters. For by many, a book is seen as the lonely product of a writer's skill, imagination, and self-discipline. However, this popular image grossly misrepresents the contributions that others make to the preparation and publication of a research study. I for one am indebted to the advice, encouragement, and support of many individuals and groups.

To the editors of *The Urban Governors* series, I am most deeply obligated. Heinz Eulau was singularly responsible for my decision to undertake and complete this study. First as a teacher, then as a dissertation adviser and project director, and finally as an editor, Heinz Eulau provided a standard of excellence—intellectual and professional—for which I will ever remain grateful. And throughout, Kenneth Prewitt steadied the study's direction, untangled sundry confusions, and patiently answered all questions.

I am also indebted to the city managers of the San Francisco Bay Area. Without their willingness to take time from crowded calendars to submit to interviews and fill out questionnaires, this study would have been little more than a discarded research design. Instead, I found the city managers to be cooperative, candid, and insightful respondents. To these men I owe a great deal for the data provided and for making the interviews a pleasant experience.

To other members of the City Council Research Project—especially Betty Zisk, Peter Lupsha, and Tom Cronin—I should note their personal and collegial assistance as the study progressed from research design to field study. Several teachers were specifically helpful when I began this project as a graduate student at Stanford University: in particular, I would thank Howard S. Becker for an interest in field work; Donald Pelz for an introduction to the possibilities and subtleties of survey research; W. Richard Scott for an analytical overview of formal organizations; and Todd LaPorte for a timely and crucial perspective on role theory.

I am also beholden to varied support from the University of California at Riverside. I would warmly thank two colleagues, Francis Carney and Charles Adrian, for their comments and occasional criticisms. Several students, among them Martin Becker, Phil Gianos, and Dan Greenberg, labored to improve what information I had and how it was expressed. And I received generous financial assistance in the form of University of California Summer Fellowships and Intramural Grants which provided the time and funds to prepare the study for publication. (My service on the Riverside City Charter Revision Commission also provided a valuable contact with the "real world" problems of the city manager and his city councilmen.)

Finally, I would express my special thanks to my wife, Marsha, for permitting the study to become a frequent and obtrusive house guest and for her willingness to act as critic, proofreader, and editor. But more than specific tasks, she created a warm and lively sanctuary for which I was continually grateful.

Despite these acknowledgments, I alone bear the responsibility for the study. For while the book is much improved by the participation of others, the errors of the study—whether in approach, content, or conclusions—are those of the author.

Ronald O. Loveridge

Contents

Tables and Illustrations

Chapter 1

Introduction

This is a study of the city manager as a political actor and his relation to the process of policy making. There are four reasons for a careful study of city managers. First, the study provides the opportunity to bring recent concerns of theory and method to bear on a favorite subject of traditional scholarship. When this study was proposed in 1963, local politics was emerging from exile in the backwaters of political science. Previously, most studies tended to be formal and prescriptive, with city politics treated "more as a matter of administration than politics."[1] Pitched at the level of specialized reporting and good government maxims, scholarship on local government attracted very little attention and had almost no influence on other political scientists. In an incisive, now classic, critique, Lawrence Herson highlighted the shortcomings of the "Lost World of Municipal Government":

> in conceptual understanding and in execution, most of the research in this field falls short of the minimal requirements for a systematic political science; for the literature of municipal government is studded with an array of facts that have been gathered with little regard for the construction of general theories; and, at the same time, it is beset with theories that have been advanced without ever being checked against available empirical data.[2]

---

[1]Edward Banfield and James Q. Wilson, *City Politics* (Cambridge, Mass.: Harvard University Press, 1963), p. 1.
[2]Lawrence Herson, "Lost World of Municipal Government," *American Political Science Review*, 51 (June 1957), 330.

At the same time, the city manager was a favorite of local government writers; for the keystone to their interpretation of local
politics was, as Herson notes, "the proposition that manager government is the best form of government."[3] In much early writing
and research, a major concern was to discuss, even prove, this
proposition—Harold Alderfer, for example, explains, "No system
is perfect, but the council-manager form allows the best possible
combination of democracy and efficiency in local government."[4]
Yet, despite frequent praise, discussion, and debate, the city manager was mainly the focus of highly descriptive research. Careful
and systematic studies were few in number, with even these show-
ing a lack of concern for the standards of proof required by
scientific analysis.[5] Therefore, this field study of the city manager
was partially conceived as an alternative to specialized reporting or
armchair prescription and, instead, is an attempt to use selected
concepts and methods from the behavioral persuasion in political
science to examine a subject for which there are many more viewpoints than rigorous empirical results.[6]

---

[3]For an excellent overview of the central place of the city manager in the
traditional study of local government, see *ibid.*, pp. 330–45.

[4]Harold Alderfer, *American Local Government and Administration* (New
York: The Macmillan Company, 1956), p. 308.

[5]The two best field studies on the city manager were completed before 1945.
The first, Leonard White's *The City Manager* (Chicago: University of Chicago
Press, 1927), was based on unstructured interviews with a "considerable
number" of city managers and short visits to thirty-one cities and offered a
thorough evaluation of the administrative and political performance of the
manager. And the second, Harold Stone, Don Price, and Kathryn Stone's *City
Manager Government in the United States* (Chicago: Public Administration
Service, 1940), a nationwide review of the results and practical operations of the
city manager plan in fifty cities, was based on composite evaluations of eighteen
cities studied by the authors and thirty-two cities studied by graduate students
or other professors. Nevertheless, though informative and seminal, the two
studies demonstrated a general disinterest in questions of theory, concept,
or method. After 1945, the city manager form was the direct focus of few
empirical studies of any consequence. The behavioral persuasion relegated
the city manager to the sidelines of community research. Questions about
the community political system, decision-making process, and leadership structure took priority over questions of efficiency and economy or of what constitutes the preferred form of local government. The city manager was seen
as one of many forces that act to mold public policy, more as another param-
eter to account for in studying the urban political environment.

[6]The behavioral persuasion has had a profound impact on American political
science. Though agreement on a precise definition of behavioralism nowhere

Second, the urban crisis underscores the importance of the city manager. For the quality, perhaps even the existence, of American society is now dependent on innovation and leadership in city politics and local public policies. As the study's problem and design took form, a profound change occurred in the conventional wisdom of political scientists, policy makers, and the attentive public. Until the 1960s, local political decisions were stereotyped as routine and inconsequential, structured by the mechanics of administration, not by the politics of choice. Typical problems were defined as where to put city trash containers or when to open the municipal pool. However, racial strife, a decline of the central city, and a concern with the quality of life forced a new awareness of the urban places where most of us live, work, and play. The so-called good life is seen as inseparable from the good city; for as Norton Long correctly observed, "The future of the metropolis is the future of most of us. The quality of life that is lived in it is the quality of American life."[7]

Third, two other developments related to the urban crisis further enhance the value of studying city managers. First—an emerging consensus among political writers contends that solutions to the problems of the city will significantly depend on innovation and leadership by the executives of local policy. For solutions to the urban crisis, scholars and the public initially looked to Washington, D.C., whether for a war on poverty, urban renewal, a model cities program, clean air, or money to kill rats. New departments such as Housing and Urban Development and

---

exists, the primary emphases include precision of data and research design and more rigorous theoretical formulations. For an interesting historical commentary, see Albert Somit and Joseph Tanenhaus, *The Development of American Political Science: From Burgess to Behavioralism* (Boston: Allyn & Bacon, 1967). As to more specific statements, this writer would recommend five useful introductions to the behavioral persuasion in political science. James Charlesworth, ed., *The Limits of Behavioralism in Political Science* (Philadelphia: American Academy of Political and Social Science, 1962); Robert Dahl, "The Behavioral Approach in Political Science: Epitaph for a Monument to a Successful Protest," *American Political Science Review*, 56 (December 1961), 763–72; Heinz Eulau, *Behavioral Persuasion in Politics* (New York: Random House, 1963); Heinz Eulau, ed., *Political Behavior in America* (New York: Random House, 1966); and Austin Ranney, ed., *Essays on the Behavioral Study of Politics* (Urbana: University of Illinois Press, 1962).

[7]Quote can be found in Eugene Lee, ed., *California Governmental Process* (Boston: Little, Brown, 1966), p. 215.

Transportation were set up. Rhetoric—if not expectation—was high that the Good Society would emerge from decisions made on the Potomac. However, the venerable Walter Lippmann was quick to address himself to these prospects: one major essay concluded that if there were to be a great society, the real work had to be done at the local level and not in the nation's capital. The same theme—that effective urban programs, regardless of the funding involved, cannot be productions of the federal government—was to be developed in the late 1960s by many other political observers; for example, Daniel Moynihan, perhaps America's best known urbanologist, concluded, "liberals must divest themselves of the notion that the nation, especially the cities of the nation, can be run from agencies in Washington."[8] The American city, central and suburb, is where motivations, conflicts, and programs are played out. Effective urban change will require immense skills and leadership at the local level. We should thus expect executives of local policy to become increasingly more important contributors to the solutions of urban problems.

And, second, many political writers also note an increasing demand as well as a probable need for direct participation in determining one's own affairs. The thrust of such action concepts as black power, student power, participatory democracy, local control, and community identity all call for new forms of political participation. In addition to the popular demand—at least among a special segment of the public, if not the general public—for personal access and political effectiveness at the local level, many of America's outstanding political writers now make the same plea. For example, Robert Dahl sees an approaching crisis in the socialization of citizens into the political life of the democratic nation-state; he writes, "What we need . . . is a political unit of more truly human proportions in which a citizen can acquire confidence and mastery of the arts of politics—that is, of the arts required for shaping a good life in common with fellow citizens."[9]

---

[8]Daniel Moynihan, "A Liberal Turn to Right?" *Los Angeles Times*, Sunday, October 1, 1967, Sec. G, p. 2, col. 1.
[9]Robert Dahl, "The City in the Future of Democracy," *American Political Science Review*, 61 (December 1967), 967.

And Richard Goodwin, former presidential adviser to John Kennedy, advocates much the same position:

> As important as the content and direction of public policies are the methods and structures used to carry them out. Initially, the elaborate structure of American federalism mirrored the judgment that a great deal should be left to local authority. For decades we have been moving in the other direction. Not only is this a dangerous and, as I believe, a mistaken course, but it is becoming clearer that certain substantive objectives utterly depend upon fashioning fresh techniques. Modern poverty, for example, cannot be abolished by friendly edicts from remote officials, and even if it could, the result would be sterile, vacuous, and purely material.
>
> The blended goal of structure and policy alike must be to meet specific ills through the methods which can in themselves enlarge the sense and reality of individual relevance and participation. The way to accomplish this, at least on the political front, is through decentralization—by assisting and compelling states, communities, and private groups to assume a greater share of responsibility for collective action. In other words, both burden and enterprise must be shifted into units of action small enough to allow for more intimate personal contact and numerous enough to widen the outlets for direct participation and control.[10]

The convergence of public demand and intellectual criticism upon a devolution of political functions and power should also work to enhance the research status of the executives of local policy.[11]

Finally, the city manager is an important local policy executive in his own right.[12] City managers are executives for a popular

---

[10]Richard Goodwin, "The Shape of American Politics," *Commentary,* 44 (June 1967), 36.

[11]It would be folly not to recognize that there are many and important forces acting to nationalize politics. Vast changes in technology, population, communication, transportation, employment, and the growth of continental organizations all guarantee that the nation-state will not wither away. Nevertheless, the emergence of participation as the action cry of the 1960s should increase the political support and therefore the resources of those local policy executives who are most accessible and visible to individual citizens.

[12]For a useful discussion of the city manager as a political administrator, see the symposium in *Public Administration Review,* 18 (Summer 1958): Charles Adrian, "A Study of Three Communities," 208–13; Dorothea Strauss Pealy, "Need for Elected Leadership," 214–16; and Karl Bosworth, "Manager is a Politician," 216–22. Many of the same points can be found in comparative case

form of local government. Appointed by a lay council to administer city hall, the city manager normally has full responsibility for the conduct of city services and the presentation of
policy issues and problems to the council. As of January 1, 1968,
city managers held such appointments in more than twenty-one
hundred American cities with a total population of over fifty
million.[13]

The city manager, however, is more than a popular administrator, for he is potentially a major policy innovator and leader.
He enters city politics as a full-time professional committed to
direct intervention in policy matters:

> To begin with, a major source of innovations are those profes-
> sional occupational roles centrally concerned with community in-
> stitutions. Part of the job of certain occupations is to constantly
> propose changes in community institutions. Such professionalized
> roles as city manager . . . carry within themselves the notion of
> constant improvement in the services involved.[14]

The prominent place of the manager in policy decisions can be
attributed to reasons beyond the career obligations of reporting
city problems and proposing policy solutions. The manager's
recognized expertise, his position at the apex of city administration, and his virtual monopoly of technical and other detailed
information propel him, willingly or unwillingly, into a pivotal
policy position. Explained briefly, city managers are, in some
manner, involved in the making, shaping, or vetoing of public
policy.[15] And this involvement in the policy process could have

studies of ten council-manager communities by Gladys Kammerer, Charles
Farris, John DeGrove, and Alfred Clubok, *The Urban Political Community:
Profiles in Town Politics* (Boston: Houghton Mifflin, 1963).
[13]*Municipal Year Book 1968* (Washington, D.C.: International City Managers'
Association), p. 133.
[14]Peter Rossi, "Theory, Research, and Practice in Community Organization,"
in *Democracy in Urban America,* Oliver Williams and Charles Press, eds. (Chicago: Rand McNally, 1961), p. 388.
[15]The city manager is an excellent example of what Charles Lindblom calls
a reconstructive leader: "policy makers have to make their policy decisions
within the constraints of existing preferences (of citizens and leaders). Over
time, however, they have many opportunities to alter the preferences that at
any given time constrain them. A leader who sees this possibility and who is
skilled enough to exploit it we shall call a reconstructive leader. He neither

important effects on the allocation of values in a community; for, as Karl Bosworth wisely observed, "Not only is he [city manager] inevitably in public view, but the range of his operations is broad, and the fate of his community may be determined in part by the public goals his thoughts lead him to set for his government."[16]

Furthermore, the city manager—now required to be innovator and leader—should assume even greater prominence in the policy process during the last quarter of the twentieth century.[17] Iola Hessler in *29 Ways to Govern a City* suggests why:

> The increasing complexity of urban problems, the rapid rate of change in the kinds of services demanded by cities, the growing dependence of government upon "experts," the mushrooming growth of electronic data processing, and developing impact of federal subsidies and controls on local governments, all require an intensification of the use of the professional in city government.[18]

The city manager should develop as a policy practitioner extraordinary, for increasingly he will become a public interpreter of problems, issues, and policies to council and community, a policy generalist among technical specialists, and a professional executive trained in handling new information and new problems.

To state that more research is needed raises the question of why. All four reasons point to the central justification: the potential if not the actual policy importance of the city manager. On the local stage, the city manager certainly acts as one of the major gatekeepers of policy innovation and leadership. And because

---

resigns himself to the constraint of preferences as he finds them, nor, on the other hand, does he necessarily attempt the impossible task of winning all other participants over to his views or preferences. He takes the middle course of shifting others' preferences so that the policies he desires fall within (whereas they formerly fell outside) the constraints imposed by the preferences of other participants in policy making. And he then uses what power or influence he has to get the policy he wants." Charles Lindblom, *The Policy-Making Process* (Englewood Cliffs, N.J.: Prentice-Hall, 1968), p. 105

[16]Bosworth, "Manager is a Politician," p. 216.

[17]See Robert Lane, "Decline of Politics and Ideology in a Knowledgeable Society," *American Sociological Review,* 31 (October 1966), 649–62.

[18]Iola Hessler, *29 Ways to Govern a City* (Cincinnati: Hamilton County Research Foundation, 1966), p. 96. See also Alexander George, "Political Leadership and Social Change in American Cities," *Daedalus,* 97 (Fall 1968), 1194–1217.

he is so strategically situated, this study assumes that the manager's policy views and activities have important effects on who
gets what, when, and how in a community.

To approach the city manager and his relation to the policy
process, this study focuses on the policy role of the city manager.
If we accept the assumption that "the behavior of all agents in
the political process is conditioned by the conception of appropriate roles for themselves,"[19] the policy role of the city manager
should be especially salient. Unlike most political executives, the
city manager has frequent occasion to think and talk about his
policy role.[20] The controversy over the proper policy role of the
city manager began with the plan's origin and has continued in
municipal literature, conferences, and ICMA (International City
Managers' Association) materials. The result is that a city manager usually has a relatively well-defined conception of what he
should do in the policy process.

The policy role is thus conceived as the link that relates the
city manager to the policy process.[21] Such a study should hope-

---

[19]Duane Lockard, *Politics of State and Local Government* (New York: The
Macmillan Company, 1963), p. 435.

[20]Note, for example, the tenor of this statement by two city managers: "The
familiar, never-answered questions concerning the philosophy of professional
city management, the proper role of the council and manager, and the dearth
of political leadership were discussed time and again." C. A. Harrell and
D. G. Weiford, "City Manager and the Policy Process," *Public Administration
Review*, 19 (Spring 1959), 102.

[21]To be candid, however, one must say that the concept *role* does not provide
a closed approach with ready-made sets of substantive propositions. Here, too,
despite conceptual popularity, there is a striking paucity of systematic empirical
research—as Donald Olmsted explains: "Social roles and related concepts have
been both exciting and exasperating to social scientists—exciting because of
the insights and theoretical linkages the terms appear to provide, and exasperating because of the severe difficulties that have been encountered in framing
pertinent and acceptable rigorous research procedures." Donald Olmsted,
Social Groups, Roles, and Leadership (East Lansing, Mich.: Michigan State
University Press, 1961), p. 33. As a partial remedy, this study builds on the research notions advanced in two major empirical role studies: Neal Gross, Ward
Mason, and Alexander McEachern, *Explorations in Role Analysis* (New York:
John Wiley & Sons, 1958), and John Wahlke, Heinz Eulau, William Buchanan,
and LeRoy Ferguson, *The Legislative System* (New York: John Wiley & Sons,
1962). These studies provide a set of concepts and methods which will be
exploited for the study of the city manager's policy role. The Gross, Mason,
and McEachern role study is perhaps the best known and most widely ap-

fully reveal shared policy expectations and values, conflicts with the council, emphases on strategies and uses of resources, as well as an overview of the behavior of the city manager in the policy process. These research areas are assumed to be central to an understanding or explanation of the city manager as an innovator and leader in city politics.

This monograph is divided into three parts. The first part discusses the general and specific context of the study. Chapter two reviews the major features, history, scholarship, and controversies surrounding the city manager. Particular attention is given to when and how the policy role emerged as a matter of controversy. Chapter three sets forth and examines the study's theoretical perspective, research procedures, and field setting. Close attention is given to the major definitions and central questions of the study.

The second part centers on the policy role in terms of intraposition consensus among city managers and interposition consensus between city managers and city councilmen. Chapter four examines the normative character of the policy role as defined by city managers; the attempt is to describe what agreements exist, to account for what differences are found, and to identify the major policy hopes and plans expressed. Chapter five explores the city councilmen's expectations of the city manager's policy role. And Chapter six presents an analysis of the interposition role conflict between city managers and city councilmen. Role disagreement looms so important that this chapter is devoted to the kind, extent, and resolution of the policy role conflicts that exist between managers and councilmen.

The third part examines the city manager as a participant in the policy process. Chapter seven addresses itself to the policy behavior of the city manager: what do we classify as policy be-

---

plauded. These authors combine an important discussion of the concept role with a careful empirical study of the role relationships between school superintendents and school boards. In political science, *The Legislative System* is probably the only comprehensive field study which systematically uses the concept of role. This study by Wahlke, Eulau, Buchanan, and Ferguson centers on the legislators of four states. This writer will borrow heavily in conception and operation from both these studies.

havior; what does a city manager do; what effect do role conceptions have; and, finally, what strategies are used and policies promoted? Chapter eight reviews and evaluates the place and importance of the city manager in community politics. Also some comment is directed toward the manager as a democratic executive and to what the future might hold.

Chapter 2

Political Executive of Good Government

Permit me to say in language as plain as I can make it that city managers have made the outstanding contribution to public administration in the United States in the 20th Century.

CHARLES MERRIAM

To the municipal reformer, the verdict is complex in cause yet simple in decision: the city is in trouble! Growth, social conflict, changing needs, and expanding services have posed unresolved problems for urban America. Urban problems, however, are not new. If today's critic had attended the first National Conference on Good Government held in 1894, he would have found the urgent problems all too familiar. Even the recommendations of that 1894 conference when compared, for example, to the Committee for Economic Development's *Modernizing Local Government* (1966), are similar in direction and underlying assumptions. Nevertheless, a fundamental difference exists because the early municipal reform movement held, in effect, constitutional conventions for the cities. Between the years 1890 and 1915, the three contemporary forms of local government emerged: strong mayor, commission, and city manager. All reforms centered on one major change: stronger executive power, keynoted on demands for efficiency and economy and lessening the power of the political boss.

The city manager plan, the last to emerge, received the pledge of allegiance of the reformers. Sanctioned in 1915 by the National

Municipal League, the plan was presented as the League's Model City Charter. In a recent pamphlet published by the League, *The Story of the Council-Manager Plan: Most Democratic and Efficient Form of Municipal Government,* the essential features of the plan are explained as follows:

1) A short ballot with few elective offices and all of them important enough to attract full public scrutiny.
2) A small council which holds all the city's power.
3) A single professional executive in charge of municipal affairs and responsible to the council.[1]

At sometimes extravagant length, every municipal textbook will expand the above description. But rather than an exact accounting of the legal arrangements, attention would be better invested in examining the distinguishing characteristics of the city manager plan. Let us review four such characteristics:[2]

1) *Unification of Power.* All powers over legislation and control of administration are vested in the city council. As contrasted to the federal model, there are no important checks or balances, no separation of powers, and no veto powers. Rather, the unification of powers, administrative and legislative, is the plan's most important legal innovation.

2) *Separation of Functions.* A city manager charter or enabling ordinances, however, attempt to establish the office, duties, and powers of the city manager so as to restrict the council's work to legislation and to place the function of administration in the hands of an appointed manager. Councilmen are instructed not to dictate appointments nor to interfere in any way with the administration of city affairs. For instance, a standard clause states, "except for the purpose of inquiry, the City Council and its members shall deal with the administrative service solely through the City Manager, and neither the City Council nor any member thereof shall give any order to any of the subordinates of the

---

[1] *The Story of the Council-Manager Plan: Most Democratic and Efficient Form of Municipal Government* (New York: National Municipal League, 1955), p. 4.
[2] The analysis of the structural features of the city manager plan draws heavily on William Anderson and Edward Weidner, *American City Government* (New York: Holt, Rinehart and Winston, 1950), pp. 380–92.

City Manager."[3] The manager is assigned a number of enumerated duties and powers, among them the powers of appointment, supervision, enforcement of laws, preparation of budget, and presentation of reports. The separation and designation of administrative responsibilities is now a cardinal conviction of managerial philosophy and is jealously guarded and advocated. Managers have taken on the obligation (or at least the threat) to resign rather than permit councils to interfere with their administrative functions.

3) *Concentration of Administrative Authority.* A single official, appointed by the council, is responsible for administering city hall. No other governmental model provides for a chief executive not subject to direct election. The hope of the reformers was to create a profession of executives trained as experts in city government.

4) *Council Control over Administration.* At the same time, the council can exercise control over the city manager through six specific sanctions: (1) power to appoint him; (2) power to dismiss him at any time; (3) power to control the purse; (4) power to pass all ordinances and resolutions, subject to no veto whatever; (5) power to investigate the manager's books and administration at any time; and (6) requirement of the manager to be present at council meetings and to answer questions about his administration. These prerogatives led Arthur Bromage to remark, "The council holds the cards in the American manager plan."[4]

Within the formal guidelines, the successes and tensions of the city manager form take shape, and thus the emergence of administrative expertise and the potential conflicts between manager and council should be readily predictable.

The city manager plan centers in an elected council limited by function to legislative matters and an appointed executive responsible for the administration of the city. Though the politics-administration dichotomy constitutes the formal heart of the city manager plan, its advocates saw the manager not merely as

---

[3]*Municipal Code,* Section 2, Ordinance 227 (1965), Concord, California, p. 11.
[4]Arthur Bromage, *Municipal Government and Administration* (New York: Appleton-Century-Crofts, 1957), p. 299.

a clerk to the council: "he was meant to exercise broad discretion in the administration of policies and to help formulate
new policies of social welfare and municipal enterprise."[5] From
the beginning, in practice as well as theory, uncertainty and tension focused on the policy role of the manager: what was he to
do? This conflict provides examples of the clash between expertise and authority, between experts and amateurs, between
cosmopolitans and locals. But let us return to the beginning.

History of the City Manager Plan

Political Form

The American urban scene between 1860 and 1910 changed
drastically under the impact of technology, migration, and rapid
economic growth. Americans in increasing numbers became city
dwellers—urban population during this fifty-year period grew
from 19.8 percent to 45.7 percent of the national total. City government, however, judged by standards of efficiency, cost, and
service was a national failure. Whether middle-class reformer or
tenement slum dweller, residents of American cities by the late
1890s had good reason to agree with the famous critique of Andrew
White, "With very few exceptions, the city governments of the
United States are the worst in Christendom—the most expensive,
the most inefficient, and the most corrupt."[6]

The harsh indictment of the cities was based on a varied catalog of ills, all compounded by accelerating industrialization and
urbanization. By the 1850s, city government, though unprepared
and ill-equipped, had assumed new responsibilities in such areas
as fire, education, police, streets, sewer, and water. These services
had to be funded, public works constructed, and franchises distributed. Major economic stakes could now be allocated by city hall.
Soon after, the city boss emerged, the practitioner of a politics of
patronage and payoffs. Two urban historians, after careful review

---

[5]Harold Stone, Don K. Price, and Kathryn Stone, *City Manager Government in
the United States* (Chicago: Public Administration Service, 1940), p. 17.
[6]Andrew White, *Forum*, 10 (December 1890), 25.

of the period, conclude, "Bossism, machine government, and corruption of public officials were typical in American cities during most of the nineteenth century."[7]

The reaction, once underway, rapidly gathered momentum. By 1880, municipal reform commanded attention in city after city. Probably no problem exercised amateur democrats more than what to do about the city. Their attention focused on municipal services, for positive government activities such as planning and welfare were as of yet largely unknown or unacceptable. While specifics varied, certain reform efforts can be identified. Two major changes centered on (1) eliminating state interference in municipal affairs, and (2) concentration of executive authority. The latter development was the harbinger of new formal arrangements of city government. Efforts at first were directed at strengthening the power of the mayor. But, to many reformers, a plan for a strong mayor seemed to embroil the city in patronage and politics and do little to facilitate the rule of experts in government. Dissatisfaction led first to the support of the commission form and then to the emergence of the manager plan.

The National Municipal League is perhaps the best register of early municipal reform. In 1894, the first National Conference on Good Government was held; out of this conference came the National Municipal League. Coordinating publicity and research, the League symbolized the consolidation of reform groups into a national movement. To concentrate executive authority, the League recommended first the Strong Mayor form (1899) and then the City Manager plan (1915). The root causes that culminated in its adoption are explained by Leonard White as follows:

> The origin of the council-manager plan is embedded in the revolution of the civic and business interests of the American city, aided and abetted by various forward-looking groups, against the waste, extravagance, and sometimes corruption which characterized "politician" government of the last century. . . . Low standards of municipal accomplishment, waste and misapplication of public

---

[7]Charles Glaab and A. Theodore Brown, *A History of Urban America* (New York: The Macmillan Company, 1967), p. 197.

funds, lack of vision with regard to the city's future and lack of
energy in pursuing even the most limited objectives, government by
political machines for the purpose of maintaining the strength and
controlling power of the machine rather than by independent officials for the good of the community, jealousy and ill will between
communities even where co-operation was essential, concealment of
the real condition of public business rather than frank recognition
of the right of the public to know the facts of public affairs—all
co-operated in varying degree to produce the discontent, distrust,
and suspicion of the mayor and council, or the commission, in most
of the 375 cities which have adopted the council-manager plan.[8]

The first large city to adopt the manager plan was Dayton,
Ohio, in 1914. The adoption was well publicized, and its city
manager proved to be unusually successful in administering an
expanded municipal program. After Dayton, cities adopted the
plan in increasing numbers. Though regarded by some as a progressive phenomenon that reached its watershed before the De-
pression, statistics do not support that interpretation. The plan
continues to show growth, with the largest increase coming after
World War II as suburban communities incorporated and chose
forms of government. Now a majority of cities with populations
between twenty-five thousand and two hundred and fifty thousand have adopted the city manager plan. And the trend toward
adoption continues in these middle-sized cities.[9]

---

[8]Leonard White, *The City Manager* (Chicago: University of Chicago Press,
1927), p. ix.
[9]The growth of the city manager plan is not randomly nor uniformly distributed throughout the United States; it differs by regions, socioeconomic
characteristics, and city size. Six states, including California, Florida, Maine,
Michigan, Pennsylvania, and Texas, have almost half of the cities which have
adopted the city manager plan. In one state, Indiana, adoption is prohibited
by state law. More generally, Raymond Wolfinger and John Field found striking
regional variations in form of government for cities of more than fifty thousand
residents: the manager plan is predominant in the West (81%), is somewhat
favored in the South (59%), is less so in the Midwest (37%), and is rather
unpopular in the Northeast (18%). See Raymond Wolfinger and John Field,
"Political Ethos and the Structure of City Government," *American Political
Science Review*, 60 (June 1966), 306–26. As to socioeconomic characteristics,
Leo Schnore and Robert Alford in perhaps the best systematic attempt to establish such differences between mayor-council, commission, and city manager
cities, conclude after an analysis of 300 suburbs, "In general, we found the
popular image of the council-manager suburb verified; it does tend to be the

The city manager form is more than a set of legal arrangements; it makes important assumptions on how good government should and will work. These assumptions emerged from various streams of reform principles, cultural values, and situational factors. And it is these assumptions which often fuel the tension, conflict, and confusion that characterize the policy role of the manager.[10]

---

natural habitat of the upper middle class. In addition, however, we found this type to be inhabited by a younger, more mobile, white population that is rapidly growing." Leo Schnore and Robert Alford, "Socioeconomic Characteristics of Suburbs," *Administrative Science Quarterly*, 8 (June 1963), 15. And Table 2–1 highlights major adoption variations by size of city. First, the city manager form has not found acceptance in large cities. See an excellent essay, Wallace Sayre, "The General Manager Idea for Large Cities," *Public Administration Review*, 14 (Autumn 1954), 253–58. And, second, as John Kessel noted, "the mayor-council system continues to dominate . . . in the small towns." John Kessel, "Governmental Structure and Political Environment," *American Political Science Review*, 56 (September 1962), 615–20.

[10]One important misconception that resulted from the national campaign for acceptance of the city manager plan should be corrected. For the early campaign efforts still influence the way in which many scholars, practitioners, and the public interpret the rationale of the city manager plan. Initial acceptance and promotion of the manager plan can largely be attributed to the genius of one man, Richard S. Childs. As executive secretary of the National Short Ballot Organization, Childs was able to place his personal ideas on the agenda for national reform. He saw the manager idea as a remedy to the principal weakness of the mayor and commission forms: the imposition of administrative duties on elected representatives and the lack of expert administration. Next, after the idea, came the immense task of persuasion. Within the reform movement, Childs and associates were almost immediately successful as the city manager plan became the approved form of good government within five years after its conception. To persuade a nation, however, the city manager plan was tied to the image of big business and its operation. Childs, for one, proposed the manager plan as a more modern version of the commission plan and self-consciously fused the "symbols of Big Business with those of the New Freedom—'business corporation,' 'board of directors,' 'popular government,' 'political responsibility.'" And with such symbols came the associated emphases on honesty and especially efficiency in government. The promotional rhetoric thus stressed business organization and practices, procedures rather than results, and administrative rather than sociopolitical goals. The impact of the city manager—business analogy was persuasive, for the appeal of more business in government was a popular and widely accepted premise during the first quarter of this century.

The fusion of the symbols of big business with the city manager form nevertheless confounded the original intent of the city manager reform. The plan represented objectives beyond a business-like form of government. The early reformers were indignant about the shame of the cities and not simply

Table 2-1
Trends in the Distribution of City Manager Plan by Population Groups: 1950, 1958, and 1966.

Population Group	1950 Cities with Manager Plan		1958 Cities with Manager Plan		1966 Cities with Manager Plan	
	Number	Percent*	Number	Percent*	Number	Percent*
Over 500,000	0	0	1	6	5	19
250,000–500,000	6	26	9	39	13	48
100,000–250,000	18	33	25	37	50	52
50,000–100,000	36	34	61	46	121	53
25,000–50,000	65	31	134	47	244	52
10,000–25,000	175	26	318	40	468	42
5,000–10,000	195	20	337	29	344	30

*Percentages are derived from total number of all cities in that population group. Data are from *Municipal Year Book(s)* published by International City Managers' Association.

Although called an elitist innovation, the municipal reform movement had as a central value the popular control of city government. A convergence of populism and progressivism gave impetus to the search for ways to make public opinion more effective in local affairs. Accepting the classic view of the rational voter, various structural devices were invented to insure that the "grass roots" public directly exercise influence on local policies, hence the advocacy of home rule, short ballot, unification of powers (to provide a target for removal and thus accountability) and, at first, proportional representation. This first assumption rested on the belief in the concerned citizen and rational voter who was to enforce decision making for the public interest in periodic elections.

Another assumption that gained acceptance was the need for expertise in government. The Jacksonian model of the spoils system, rotation, and inexpertness in office came under heavy attack. Agreement developed that the complicated task of city administration demanded trained professionals. Good government advocates opted for ways that the city experts could be independent of, or at least not dependent on, political changes. This second assumption that good government is in some measure premised on expertise not directly tied to political events is an axiom of the city-manager plan.

No reform principle received more attention and exhortation than the strengthening of the executive. Those who drew up the city manager plan likewise sought to increase the discretion and prerogatives of the chief executive, namely, the city manager. "The position of city manager," wrote Richard Childs in 1915, "is the central feature of the plan."[11] But given the unification of authority and final responsibility in the council, the question immediately arose of how to make sure the councilmen would

concerned with how to balance the budget or account for city expenditures. They did not envision the city manager as a neutral, efficient administrative technician; instead, they hoped to create a strong executive who would formulate and propose new policies of social welfare and municipal enterprise as well as exercise broad administrative discretion. See Don Price, "The Promotion of the City Manager Plan," *Public Opinion Quarterly*, 5 (Winter 1941), 563–78.
[11]Richard Childs, "How the Commission-Manager Plan Is Getting Along." *National Municipal Review*, 4 (July 1915), 373.

give the city manager a chance to perform as a chief executive. The answer proposed and what now has become common practice was to spell out and distinguish manager functions from council functions. This division of functions between manager and council attempted to stake out the powers and executive role of the manager.

The division of labors between manager and council is formally premised on the dichotomy between administration and politics. The city manager was to be the administrator, the council the policy maker—or so the Model Charter said. This dichotomy was embraced by many early political scientists as sound causal and normative theory. In the late 1890s, Frank Goodnow, for example, wrote:

> It is possible to distinguish in all forms and grades of government two ultimate or primary functions. The one consists in the determination of the public policy; the other in the execution of that policy after it has been once determined. The one function is legislation; the other administration. This distinction of governmental functions has been made from an early time and is at the basis of that fundamental principle of American constitutional law usually referred to as the principle of the separation of powers.[12]

The administration-politics dichotomy suffered in practice a quick and rude demise. Even at their first meeting in 1914, the city managers debunked the division of labor and spoke out in favor of executive leadership. They found—for reasons we shall discuss shortly—that it is impossible for the manager to avoid involvement in the public policy process. Nevertheless, the dichotomy is still found in all charters or enabling ordinances, and the manager continues to be popularly represented as the administrator.

The underlying assumption is one of politics that stresses consensus over cleavage. Rather than expecting conflict over the

---

[12]Frank Goodnow, "The Place of the Council and of the Mayor in the Organization of Municipal Government–the Necessity of Distinguishing Legislation from Administration," *A Municipal Program* (New York: National Municipal League, 1900), p. 74.

allocation of values, reformers thought that a wise and "public regarding" council with expert advice would reach decisions in the public interest. It has been said that one of the fundamental principles of the city manager form was the idea that "the most capable and public-spirited citizens should serve on the governing body as representatives of the city to determine policies for the benefit of the community as a whole." This interpretation rests on the classic democratic belief that men of goodwill can agree through face-to-face discussion on the common good. "Their assumptions about human nature," writes Robert Wood about the reformers, "were in the Town Meeting tradition. Men living together in the same area had, by and large, common goals for their community. Ideological issues in municipal elections were contrived and artificial, for 'good city government is good housekeeping' and that is the sum of the matter. The only division of interest was between 'good and bad,' and the majority of the citizens wanted the same results—adequate services honestly provided."[13]

Political Critique

First evaluations were almost uniformly favorable. Praise came from almost every student of public administration or local government: for example, "by their unflinching devotion to their job," wrote Leonard White, "city managers have furnished the American cities with a new and finer conception of official duty."[14] And, concluded Harold Stone, "they [city managers] added to the prestige of city government, lessened its preoccupation with trivial details or factional interests, and increased its ability to render service to the public."[15] The city manager plan became an honored political institution with its legitimacy as a political doctrine established by adoption and performance.

After World War II, however, the city manager plan was subject to heavy doses of criticism as well as praise. Several of the

---

[13]Robert Wood, *Suburbia* (Boston: Houghton Mifflin, 1958), p. 51.
[14]Leonard White, *City Manager*, p. 306.
[15]Stone, Price, and Stone, *City Manager Government*, p. 261.

original assumptions failed in practice or fell before the advances of scholarship. No assumption was more frequently debunked than the dichotomy between administration and politics. And, with its rejection, the city manager plan was open to close evaluation and review. While generally ignoring problems of administration, political observers especially criticized the policy values and supposed behavior of the city manager. The recurring themes in most of the critiques are that the city manager exerts little or no policy leadership on nonroutine decisions, is unresponsive to the needs and demands of the people, and in general acts to depoliticize the allocation of city values.

A corollary development has been the assault on the catchwords of the municipal reform movement—honesty and efficiency and the middle-class bias they are said to represent. The question asked today is rather efficiency for what? To the remark, "There is no Republican or Democratic way to pave the streets," William Lee Miller offers an engaging yet representative reply:

> Before Lee became mayor there were good-government people who would apply the slogan to New Haven, and with that larger meaning. How wrong they were! There are questions of policy with respect to paving the streets. Should the streets be paved or the money saved? Or spent on something else? Which streets? In which district? Local government in a city of any size is not mere routine or a merely 'technical' or 'administrative' matter, manageable by 'business methods.' It is a conflict of interests—and of values. Policy, we may say, is a line of action connecting the facts of a situation to some large set of values. It is the evaluative aspect that distinguishes 'policy' from administration and technique.[16]

Almost all critics focus on the original assumptions of the city manager form and gleefully demolish these.[17] Few, however, investigate what happens in practice. Obviously, the early advocates of the plan overestimated the importance of governmental

---

[16]William Lee Miller, *Fifteenth Ward and the Great Society* (Boston: Houghton Mifflin, 1966), pp. 200–201.
[17]An outstanding example of this genre is John East's vigorous but thoroughly one-sided critique of the political philosophy of Richard S. Childs. See John East, *Council-Manager Government: The Political Thought of Its Founder, Richard S. Childs* (Chapel Hill: University of North Carolina Press, 1965).

institutions as contrasted to cultural, social, and situational factors. But it is a battle too easily won; rather we should ask how does the city manager act in the real world of city politics.

City Manager Process: Plan in Practice

It has become a cliché to say that the manager is the appointed chief executive of a city. But as an accurate description, much of the meaning is lost as the phrase is solemnly repeated in textbook after textbook. We have to ask: what does a city manager do? How are these activities involved in the authoritative allocation of values? For the executive activities of the manager are the reasons why the manager inevitably participates in policy decisions and political choices.[18] The executive role can analytically be divided into three main functions: coordinator, allocator, and policy maker. Each of these activities is in itself important and influences how values are distributed in a community.

Policy Maker

The manager as chief administrator makes major staff appointments and is accountable for a wide-ranging city operation. The normal bevy of city departments includes those of planning, public works, police, parks and recreation, and finance. By necessity, the city manager has to become a jack-of-all-trades, at least to the extent that he can ask the right questions, evaluate performances and proposals, and coordinate the work of divergent

[18]There should be no question that the city manager is a major policy participant; B. James Kweder in a study of twenty-one North Carolina cities found, "The perceptions of managers, mayors, and councilmen of the policy-making process in their cities clearly refute the idea that policy making is something performed exclusively by the council. Not only do the managers participate actively in the process, they participate actively in every one of the six phases into which the policy-making process has been divided for this study. Moreover, in many cities the manager clearly emerges as the person who has the greatest influence over what is happening at every stage of the policy-making process." James Kweder, *The Roles of the Manager, Mayor, and Councilmen in Policy Making* (Chapel Hill: University of North Carolina Press, 1965), p. 31.

city departments. And he has to have an informed opinion on most major questions or problems that might be raised at council meetings. As coordinator, the quality and morale of city staff will be critical to formulation as well as implementation of policy and to the kinds of services rendered by the city. A good planning department could mean the difference between extensive and far-reaching general plans or a technician's approach to zoning requests. Or, to take another example, a good police force could mean the difference between riots or favorable minority relations. How well the city performs will determine in part what tax levels will be approved, even what new businesses might choose to locate there. To no small extent, especially in newer cities, the life style and image of the city may be importantly shaped by the way the city manager shepherds its services and policies.

Within limits, the city manager is instrumental in the distribution of available public resources. For one, city managers have established considerable autonomy in preparing budgets. In most cases, the city manager and his staff will prepare a budget without direct consultation with councilmen. Thus, the end result is pretty much a fait accompli endorsement by the council. And, as Stone explained, "The most important municipal policy is embodied in the budget, and the city manager, of course, must prepare and propose the budget."[19] Perhaps equally important, the city manager has discretionary authority to make a number of seemingly modest but, in effect, no less important allocation decisions. To illustrate, should the city purchase additional parks; if so, where should they be located; and how and when should they be developed? Or should ten new policemen be hired or should the money be spent for computational equipment? Although limited by factors such as tradition and resources, the manager has to make various decisions which are largely open to personal discretion and which in total can have a profound impact on the distribution of public resources in a community.

If we define policy making as initiation, fixing priorities, and bargaining, as well as legitimating and implementing public policy decisions, every city manager is, of course, a policy maker.

---

[19]Stone, Price, and Stone, *City Manager Government,* p. 246.

The policy participation of the manager began as soon as the first appointment was made; for it is impossible for a city manager to escape major involvement. If nothing else, an essential part of his job is to prepare and propose policy. In 1927, Leonard White clearly expressed what later studies have documented:

> Observation of managers at work leads the writer to the conviction that many, if not indeed most managers, do in fact possess the initiative in most matters of policy. One manager, who is careful to avoid any appearance of pushing himself forward, frankly said that 99 percent of council business originated with him or with officials under his control. This is not only substantially true in most cities which have been visited in the course of this study, but in my judgment must be taken as a normal situation. The office of the city manager has become the great center of initiating and proposing (but not deciding) public policies as well as the sole responsible center of administration.[20]

The manager—at the center of communications for the staff and city business—is a gatekeeper of information, advice, and consultation on city affairs. And, as often suggested, he is probably the one local actor able and expected to take a comprehensive view of the public interest and to exercise an important influence on other policy participants. Thus, a city manager's intimate involvement in the policy process, the requirement that he decide among various programs and purposes, and the influence his decisions may have on the interests within the community all contribute to making him a major political actor.

Community Leader

Though not anticipated by the original founders nor discussed by its advocates, the functional requirements of the plan

---

[20]Leonard White, *City Manager,* p. 210. Almost every study that has examined the policy behavior of the city manager agrees on three basic propositions. First, most city managers are important sources of policy innovation and leadership; and all managers are involved in the making, shaping, or vetoing of policy proposals. Second, most city managers in some measure exercise political leadership; and all city managers occupy an important political position in the community. And, third, most city councils fail to exercise much political leadership; however, the attitudes of city councils condition the political behavior of the city manager.

also thrust the city manager forward as a community leader.[21]
The expectation that a manager should be an inconspicuous,
expert errand boy for the council could not square with the facts
of community political life. For it is difficult for an amateur
council, meeting only a few hours a week, to act as an articulator
of problems or issues, much less act as a broker for conflicting
political interests or the general planner for a rapidly changing
environment.[22] The manager's emergence as a community leader
has been recognized, even endorsed, by the International City
Managers' Association (ICMA). When the ICMA Code of Ethics
was revised in 1952, the city manager was urged to be a community leader and the classic dichotomy between politics and
administration was all but repudiated:

> The city manager as a community leader submits policy proposals
> to the council and provides the council with facts and advice on
> matters of policy to give the council a basis for making decisions
> on community goals. The city manager defends municipal policies
> publicly only after consideration and adoption of such policies by
> the council.
>
> The city manager realizes that the council, the elected repre-
> sentatives of the people, is entitled to the credit for the establish-
> ment of municipal policies. The city manager avoids coming in
> public conflict with the council on controversial issues. Credit or
> blame for policy execution rests with the city manager.

If these ethical principles are read closely, the ICMA has endorsed a strong leadership role for the manager in the community.

---

[21]To this point of the city manager as a community leader, Hugo Wall explains, "The city manager of today, because of his experience, because of his
record of achievement, and because of his position at the center of the flow
of information concerning urban problems, inescapably finds himself in a
position of community leadership." Hugo Wall, "Changing Role of the City
Manager," *Public Management*, 41 (January 1959), 4.

[22]The inability and often unwillingness of councilmen to assume major innovative or leadership responsibilities has been widely documented. For example, Kweder writes, "Few of them [councilmen] initiate policy, most of
them follow the lead of either the mayor or manager, or both in making policy
decisions, and rarely do any of them take strong exception to the situation in
which they find themselves." Kweder, *Roles of the Manager, Mayor, and Councilmen*, p. 80. See also a short, well-written field study that makes the same
point. James Wilson and Robert Crowe, *Managers in Maine* (Brunswick, Maine:
Bureau for Research–Municipal Government, 1962), especially pp. 3–25.

The literature on community politics and power casts further light on the city manager as a community leader.[23] In an ambitious study of Syracuse, New York, Freeman and associates found that the most active individuals in major community decisions are government administrators.[24] This finding should not be surprising because a primary function of many top level government people is to participate in community decisions —they possess the resources of time, control over information, esteem, legitimacy, and rights pertaining to public office. But, more significantly the Syracuse study concluded that different kinds of methods discover different community leaders. Four such methods are examined: participation, reputation, position, and social activity.[25] Noteworthy is that city managers would probably be located among the top leadership by each method.

---

[23]In the 1950s and 1960s, studies of community politics and power proliferated to the extent that a specific listing would exhaust the reader's patience. Instead, anyone interested would profitably begin with several excellent reading collections and literature surveys: Terry Clark, *Community Structure, Power, and Decision Making: A Comparative Analysis* (San Francisco: Chandler Publishing Company, 1968); Willis Hawley and Frederick Wirt, *Search for Community Power* (Englewood Cliffs, N.J.: Prentice-Hall, 1968); Charles Press, *Main Street Politics* (Lansing, Mich.: Institute for Community Development, Michigan State University, 1962); and John Walton, "Substance and Artifact: The Current Status of Research on Community Power Structure," *American Journal of Sociology*, 71 (January 1966), 430–38. For a more general introduction to community studies, see a brilliant summary interpretation by Norton Long, "Political Science and the City," in *Urban Research and Policy Planning*, Lee Schnore and Henry Fagin, eds. (Beverly Hills, Calif.: Sage Publications, 1967), pp. 243–62.

[24]Linton Freeman, Thomas Fararo, Warner Bloomberg, and Morris Sunshine, "Locating Leaders in Local Communities," *American Sociological Review*, 28 (October 1963), 791–98.

[25]An extensive literature exists on how appropriate the four methods are to investigating community decision making. See, for example, Thomas Anton, "Power, Pluralism, and Local Politics," *Administrative Science Quarterly*, 7 (March 1963), 448–57; Charles Bonjean and David Olson, "Community Leadership: Directions of Research," *Administrative Science Quarterly*, 9 (December 1964), 278–95; Delbert C. Miller, "Democracy and Decision-Making in the Community Power Structure," in *Power and Democracy in America*, William D'Antonio and Howard Ehrlich, eds. (Notre Dame: University of Notre Dame, 1961), pp. 25–73; Nelson Polsby, *Community Power and Political Theory* (New Haven: Yale University Press, 1963) ; John Walton, "Discipline, Method, and Community Power: A Note on the Sociology of Knowledge," *American Sociological Review*, 31 (October 1966), 684–89; and Raymond Wolfinger, "Reputation and Reality in the Study of Community Power," *American Sociological Review*, 25 (October 1960), 636–44.

Because of his wide-ranging policy activities and high public visibility, participation and reputation measures would find the city manager at the top of the power structure. Likewise, position measures would show similar results because the city manager is the administrative head of city hall. And social activity measures should disclose the city manager to be a member of the most important civic groups. Therefore, regardless of approach, few could seemingly challenge the proposition that city managers engage in behavior resulting in determinative roles in community decision making.

But these comments are deductive and assertive; what have field studies found? Unfortunately, few of the major studies on community power have examined cities with city managers. And among the few, Ritchie Lowry's *Who's Running This Town,* for example, notes that Chico, California, has the city manager form but never again specifically mentions the office or its occupants— much less its functional consequences for politics in the community. Only two major community studies have detailed the place and role of the manager in politics: Aaron Wildavsky's *Leadership in a Small Town* and Oliver Williams and Charles Adrian's *Four Cities.* Wildavsky's study of decision making in Oberlin, Ohio (population 6,000), focuses on case histories ("every single decision of any importance from November 1957 to June 1961"). Two leaders are singled out for special comment and a chapter is devoted to each: one a councilman, the other the city manager. In closing his chapter on the manager, Wildavsky concludes:

> The City Manager is interested, active, and has the resources of his office with which to influence the course of decision-making. He is, after all, the only individual in town whose full-time job it is to help make decisions over a wide range of community affairs. Other city employees are specialized to the particular areas in which they work and they lack his formal powers and his broad contacts. . . . As a matter of course, therefore, we would expect a city manager who takes a broad view of his responsibilities, in a town without full-time elected officials, to be the most general activist and to appear in more decision areas than anyone else.[26]

---

[26]Aaron Wildavsky, *Leadership in a Small Town* (Towowa, N.J.: Bedminster Press, 1964), p. 234.

The city manager, however, is selective, according to Wildavsky, in which decisions he becomes heavily involved, and, in general, he avoids controversial decisions that have not achieved community consensus and are outside the effective purview of his office. Success was explained by "Skill in coalition building . . . [in which the city manager] proposed policies meeting widespread preferences, recruited personnel to promote them, provided a rationale for those who chose to agree, and modified opposition where necessary without giving up essential elements of their program."[27] Therefore, Wildavsky would say that time, skill, expertise, energy, information, and ability to pyramid resources establish city managers as community leaders.

Williams and Adrian in a study of four middle-sized manager cities focus more on roles of government than on decision making, more on ideology than case histories. To explain differences in policy outcomes and political styles, Williams and Adrian see a combination of factors as important: political culture, governmental structure, situational factors of strategy, and specific activity of individuals and groups. What about the city manager: how does he fit into the political outcomes of a community? The authors find no consistent pattern:

> In Beta and Gamma, the manager was a key leadership figure and a policy innovator. In Alpha he had a vigorous council, which itself sought to lead, and which shared policy making with him. In fact, his role as a leader was preserved there mostly by the deliberate intent of a council that was strongly committed to the principle of professional administration. In Delta, the council would not permit the manager to serve as either leader or innovator. Its Jeffersonian philosophy emphasized the desirability of decentralized decision-making and minimized the role of the professional administrators, including the manager.[28]

Yet, they also observe, "Rule by amateurs is likely to mean that under most conditions, persons outside the legislative body must be depended upon to make the essential policy decisions in all but a formal sense." And the city manager is typically the most

---

27*Ibid.*
28Oliver Williams and Charles Adrian, *Four Cities* (Philadelphia: University of Pennsylvania Press, 1963), p. 208.

prominent outsider. Thus, in the cities studied by Wildavsky and Williams and Adrian, the city manager appears as a policy innovator and leader of the first order.[29]

Policy Role: Controversy and Central Questions

If only an administrator, the city manager would be of intrinsic importance because of the focal position he occupies in city government. However, legal statements to the contrary, the city manager cannot avoid participation in policy decisions and, in the broadest sense, community politics. The city manager is not only responsible for the city staff but is directly accountable to the city council and indirectly to community groups, the public-at-large, and his professional colleagues. And in all his activities, the manager plays "important roles in policy innovation and leadership, in public relations, and in a role secondary to that of the mayor in ceremony functions."[30]

---

[29]At least two societal trends indicate that the city manager will probably continue as a major community influential. For one, the city offers an increasingly baffling, complex environment that the layman cannot understand or control. It is a truism that the vast technological, economic, and social changes will require and in turn place in the community limelight innovative and highly skilled policy executives. See, for example, Herman Kahn and Anthony Wiener, *The Year 2000* (New York: The Macmillan Company, 1967). And, second, the ideology of the municipal reformer has changed, so that support for the city manager plan cannot be evaluated in the terms and premises developed some fifty years ago. Robert Agger and his associates found that the ideology which best describes an increasing number of community leaders in America is that of Community Conservationism. The values attributed to this ideological outlook are as follows: "Community Conservationists value professionally trained public administrators and stress public planning; they tend to hold in disrepute the professional politician and dirty politics. They are the most recent of a long line of 'reformers,' but differ in at least one major aspect: earlier reformers tended to concentrate on eliminating particular evils so that the political system might return to a sort of laissez-faire operation in cooperation with private institutions. The Community Conservationist, in contrast, stresses the need for and duty of the government to provide long-range planning in the public interest by nonpolitical administrators. Robert Agger, Daniel Goldrich, and Bert Swanson, *The Rulers and the Ruled* (New York: John Wiley & Sons, 1964), p. 25. If an accurate description of the ideology of today's urban leadership, support for the city manager plan should continue; for the values of the Community Conservationists are quite close to those formally espoused by most city managers and their professional bodies.

[30]Charles Adrian, *State and Local Government* (New York: McGraw-Hill, 1960), p. 280.

In sum, the city manager must strive to be a complete politician as well as an effective administrator: "The city manager is among other things, chief administrator, chief legislator, political chief, symbolic and ceremonial head of the community, chief of public safety, and chief negotiator with other governments. And to be successful in these roles he must be an effective persuader, constantly using his various wiles to get his points across and action taken. He may have to bargain, accept compromises, plead for what he can get when he can't get what he wants, defer action until time is ripe, and choose well which role to play when."[31]

But the policy activities of innovation and leadership are not legally sanctioned. As a result of the difference between the faith and practice of the city manager plan, the policy role of the manager has become a cauldron of differing exhortations, descriptions, and evaluations. That the city manager can have an impact on the "allocation of values" is no longer contested. The real question is not whether but how a city manager participates in the policy process.[32] Therefore, the controversy centers on the policy role of the manager: What are the policy values of the manager? What happens to these values in practice? What difference can a city manager make? And what will be the future prospects of the city manager?[33]

---

[31]Duane Lockard, *Politics of State and Local Government* (New York: The Macmillan Company, 1963), p. 360.

[32]See an important essay, John Pfiffner, "Policy Leadership—For What?" *Public Administration Review*, 19 (Spring 1959), 121–24.

[33]Besides a general analysis of policy views, variations in manager values and behavior should obviously be studied. The authors of a twenty-year-old, yet still remarkably accurate, research design explain: "From casual observation it has been noted that once the plan is established various patterns of interaction emerge; in one city, for example, the councilmen will regard the manager as the public leader and chief executive of the city whose removal would almost constitute an act of revolution; in another, he will be considered as a chief administrator carrying out broad public policies laid down by the council; in still another, he will be a glorified errand boy, expected to keep his name out of the papers and not to speak until spoken to. We do not know what factors or personality, *what tradition, what concepts of responsibility produce these variations in behavior.*" (Emphasis is that of this writer.) Inter-university Summer Seminar on Political Behavior, Social Science Research Council, "Research in Political Behavior," *American Political Science Review*, 46 (December 1952), 1011, 1009–1015.

Chapter 3

Questions, Concepts, and Methods

The policy role of the city manager is in no way a virgin topic. Commentaries—descriptive and speculative—are nearly inexhaustible; for controversy began with the origins of the city manager plan and has continued unabated. Yet, careful inquiries into the proper policy activities and goals of the city manager are noticeably few in number. This study is based on survey research in the San Francisco Bay Area. From interview and questionnaire data, this study describes, explains, and to some extent evaluates the city manager, his policy role, and his relation to city politics. Noteworthy, a focus on the policy role is particularly well suited to scientific research, for policy views can be readily tapped by asking managers and councilmen.[1]

Five questions direct the study's research objectives. *First, how do city managers define their policy role?* City managers occupy the focal position. Their conceptions of what a city manager should do obviously provide the central content of the policy role.

Second, how do city councilmen define the policy role of the city manager? No other is more concerned about or important to the city manager's policy role than the city councilman. For the city manager, unlike most political executives, is appointed and serves at the pleasure of the council. The dependence of the

---

[1]See rationale of authors of *The Legislative System* for relying on questioning to collect data on role conceptions: John Wahlke, Heinz Eulau, William Buchanan, and LeRoy Ferguson, *The Legislative System* (New York: John Wiley & Sons, 1962), especially pp. 31–33.

manager on council approval guarantees councilmen a prominent place in defining what a city manager should do.

Third, what conflicts exist in the definition of the policy role between city managers and city councilmen? Is there disagreement? If so, what is the extent and nature of the disagreement? And what is the significance of such disagreement for the city manager's participation in the policy process?

Fourth, what is the policy role behavior of the city manager? How does the city manager participate in the policy process? What effect do policy role views have on his policy behavior? What resources does a city manager have to influence policy decisions? And what strategies can he use to influence their content?

And, fifth, what is the importance of the city manager for city politics? Administrator or community leader? Technocrat or democrat? What does—and can—the city manager do as a community leader? Finally, what does the future seem to hold for the place of the city manager in city politics?

Approach

In the local government literature, the policy role of the manager has been the frequent subject of exhortation, description, and controversy. A long list of prerogatives, requirements, values, functions, behaviors, and conceptions have been widely discussed and disputed. The term policy role appears so often that one first becomes weary, then disturbed, by its constant use. For the concept of policy role is overused and, in any scientific sense, misused.[2]

---

[2]The comments of two sociologists on the concept of role are pointedly relevant: "The concept role is at present still rather vague, nebulous, and non-definitive. Frequently in the literature, the concept is used without any attempt on the part of the writer to define or delimit the concept, the assumption being that both writer and readers will achieve an immediate compatible consensus. Concomitantly, the concept is found frequently in popular usage which adds further confusion." Lionel Neiman and James Hughes, "The Problem of the Concept of Role–A Re-Survey of the Literature," *Social Forces,* 30 (June 1951), 149.

The concept role is among the most widely used ideas in the social sciences. Although variety is the watchword in definition and development, certain general features of role theory can be highlighted.[3] These features suggest the theoretical utility of role concepts: society is conceived as a system of positions. With every position there are associated sets of expectations concerning appropriate behavior (for the position's occupant). These expectations constitute, more or less, a behavioral model, providing the occupant with values and meanings to adjust and guide his own behavior. To the extent that the occupant conforms to these expectations, he permits another person to anticipate his behavior and thus enables interacting individuals to function collectively.[4]

The three central concepts of role theory are position, role, and

---

[3]Congruent with the so-called action orientation (theory, framework), the concept of role is especially prominent in American sociology, social psychology, and cultural anthropology. Important summaries of the concept role can be found in Neal Gross, Ward Mason, and Alexander McEachern, *Explorations in Role Analysis* (New York: John Wiley & Sons, 1958), pp. 11–69; Theodore Sarbin, "Role Theory," in *Handbook of Social Psychology I,* Gardner Lindzey, ed. (Reading, Mass.: Addison-Wesley, 1954), pp. 223–58; and Bruce Biddle and Erwin Thomas, eds., *Role Theory* (New York: John Wiley & Sons, 1966). Two useful introductions to the relationship of expectations and behavior can be found in Robert Bierstedt, *Social Order* (New York: McGraw-Hill, 1957) and Arnold Rose, ed., *Human Behavior and Social Process* (Boston: Houghton-Mifflin, 1962). More seminal works on the implication of the concept role include George Mead, *Mind, Self, and Society* (Chicago: University of Chicago Press, 1934), Ralph Linton, *Study of Man* (New York: Appleton, Century, 1936), and Talcott Parsons, *Social System* (Glencoe, Ill.: The Free Press, 1951). [4]The promise of role analysis lies therefore in its attempt to explain regular and repetitive behavior by providing a linkage between the individual and the political system. The potential usefulness of the concept role is well summarized by Heinz Eulau: "It [role] is a concept generic to all the social sciences. On the social level, it invites inquiry into the structure of the interaction, connection, or bond that constitutes a relationship. On the cultural level, it calls attention to the norms, expectations, rights, and duties that sanction the maintenance of the relationship and attendant behavioral patterns. And, on the personal level, it alerts research to the idiosyncratic definitions of the role held by different actors in the relationship. Role is clearly a concept consistent with the analytic objectives of the behavioral sciences. It lays bare the inter-relatedness and inter-dependence of people." Heinz Eulau, *Behavioral Persuasion in Politics* (New York: Random House, 1963), p. 40. See also Donald Olmsted, *Social Groups, Roles, and Leadership* (East Lansing, Mich.: Michigan State University Press, 1961), especially pp. 21–35.

expectation. For the purposes of this study, the following definitions will be employed:[5]

position: a location of an actor or class of actors in a system of social relations.

role: a more-or-less integrated subset of expectations that can be distinguished from other sets of expectations applied to the same position.

expectation: an evaluative standard applied to how the occupant of a position ought to behave in a given role.

Two characteristics are worth noting: role is conceived (1) as part of a social position and (2) not as the expression of the position in action. Diagrammatically, the concepts can be represented as follows:

Position

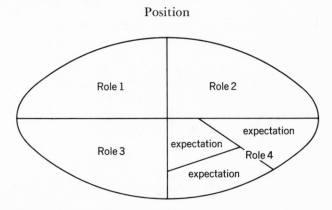

How the role structure of a position can be determined is a major problem of analysis.[6] This study adopts a functional

---

[5]The definitions are developed specifically from Frederick Bates, "Position, Role and Status: A Reformulation of Concepts," *Social Forces*, 35 (May 1956), 313–21; and more generally from Gross et al., *Explorations in Role Analysis*, pp. 48–67; and Wahlke et al., *Legislative System*, pp. 3–28, 237–44.

[6]That expectations applied to a position are not a random collection but can themselves be ordered is a generally accepted notion. This is particularly true with role analysts concerned with empirical research. For example, Gross et al., in *Explorations in Role Analysis*, called the problem role segmentation. The authors contend that in research the holistic conception of role should be

scheme, focused on what the occupant should do (or does) in that position. The major functions associated with a position are classified as pertaining to roles. Probably the most important research strategy question is the level of abstraction to use in identifying roles. Should, for example, the language of the city manager be used to express the role functions or should a more analytic and abstract language be used? Two models, among others, stand out.

A (Manager Language Model)

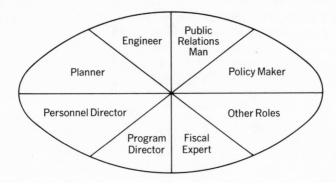

B (Analytical Model)

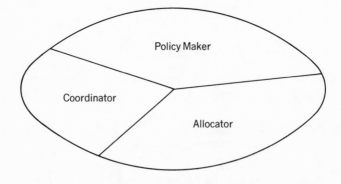

abandoned in favor of a role segment conception: "The expectations which describe role can be categorized into role segments and in empirical analysis it is also necessary to say what segments are under examination" (p. 64).

Model *B* is being chosen because of the decision to examine expectations in terms of general functions. But for other research efforts, Model *A* could be usefully employed.[7]

The assumption is sometimes made that there is a clearly defined and agreed upon set of expectations associated with a position. Empirical studies, however, consistently reveal this assumption to be suspect:

> It is a common assumption that the structural requirements for any position are as a rule defined with a high degree of explicitness, clarity, and consensus among all the parties involved. To take the position of hospital nurse as an example: it is assumed that her role-requirements will be understood and agreed upon by the hospital administration, the nursing authorities, the physicians, etc. Yet one of the striking research findings in all manner of hospitals is the failure of consensus regarding the proper role of nurse. Similar findings have been obtained in school systems, business firms, and the like.[8]

As for the city manager, evidence also indicates that he does not occupy a position for which there are clear and uncontested sets of expectations. Rather, the policy role, among others, is subject to differing definitions and interpretations. The research problem becomes how to identify expectations for the manager's policy role.

Yet before reviewing procedures, three common difficulties in role analysis merit comment. The first problem is that of multiple positions. The city manager occupies many positions in society that could be viewed as potential sources for policy expectations. Some positions such as regional officer in the ICMA or local secretary of the Chamber of Commerce could be important; others such as member of the board of directors of the local art associa-

---

[7]A rationale for *A* can be found in Gladys Kammerer, "Role Diversity of City Managers," *Administrative Science Quarterly*, 8 (March 1964), especially 428; the rationale for *B* is developed by Talcott Parsons, "Suggestions for a Sociological Approach to the Theory of Organizations–I," *Administrative Science Quarterly*, 1 (June 1956), especially 74–80.

[8]Daniel Levinson, "Role, Personality, and Social Structure," in *Sociological Theory*, Lewis Coser and Bernard Rosenberg, eds. (2nd ed.; New York: The Macmillan Company, 1964), p. 286.

tion or leader of a boy scout troop—assuming a city manager would
have the time, which he usually does not—are probably relatively
unimportant. Nevertheless, for the policy role, the occupational
position should be the major source of expectations. First, of
the various positions a manager holds, his occupation is probably
the most important determinant of his opinions and behavior.[9]
Second, the focus of the study is not on personal life style but
on the city manager as city manager. And, third, the occupational
position is in a formal organization, namely, city government.
Applicable then to the city manager is Herbert Simon's observation, "The values and objectives that guide individual decisions
in organization are largely the organizational objectives . . . the
participant in organization acquires an 'organization personality'
rather distinct from his personality as an individual."[10]

Position set is a second problem. The city manager interacts
with incumbents of many other positions, for example, members
of the council, city staff, public-at-large, community groups, professional associations, and so forth.[11] This study of the city manager's policy role, however, will focus on the manager's general
functional expectations and will not—except for the city council
—break down his expectations into more specific policy relationships. Inclusive in content, the policy role will, for research purposes, represent the manager's "attempt to structure his social
reality, to define his place within it, and to guide his search for
meaning and gratification."[12] Further, it will be assumed that
the city manager is more or less consistent in his policy role expectations, relationships, and behavior.

A third problem is role indeterminacy. Some writers have criticized role analysis because the expectational map carried around
in the head is a very rough, approximate map. Two points should
be made. First, the city manager position is an office as contrasted

---

9See Raymond Mack, "Occupational Ideology and the Determinant Role,"
Social Forces, 36 (October 1957), 37–38.
10Herbert Simon, *Administrative Behavior* (2nd ed.; Glencoe, Ill.: The Free
Press, 1957), p. 198.
11The notion of position set was formally introduced and developed by Robert
Merton, "Role Set: Problems in Sociological Theory," *British Journal of Sociology,* 8 (June 1957), 106–20.
12Levinson, "Role, Personality, and Social Structure," p. 292.

to a culturally validated status. The significance of this difference is suggested by Kingsley Davis:

> The term status would then designate a position in the general institutional system, recognized and supported by the entire society, spontaneously evolved rather than deliberately created, rooted in folkways and mores. Office, on the other hand, would designate a position in a deliberately created organization, governed by specific and limited rules in a limited group, more generally achieved than ascribed.[13]

And, second, as will be detailed later, there is among city managers a high awareness, if not agreement, on most aspects of the policy role.[14] Moreover, because the policy role is repeatedly discussed in graduate school, at conferences, in municipal literature, and so forth, city managers have self-consciously considered what the proper policy role of the city manager should be. The study is able, therefore, to focus on more or less clear—in contrast to blurred—role expressions.[15]

Procedures

The study—as the editors' preface points out—was begun under the auspices of the City Council Research Project, Institute of Political Studies, at Stanford University. The Project is investigating legislative politics in local government. The dominance of the executive in most legislative arenas made a study of the city manager a problem of special consequence, whether to the description, explanation, or evaluation of the local policy process.

---

[13]Kingsley Davis, *Human Society* (New York: The Macmillan Company, 1948), pp. 88–89.

[14]See Jeptha Carrell, *Role of the City Manager* (Kansas City, Mo.: Community Studies, 1962), pp. 5–21; or Clarence Ridley, *The Role of the City Manager in Policy Formulation* (Chicago: International City Managers' Association, 1958), pp. 7–22.

[15]For role analysis, the importance of clear role conceptions can be seen in the results of Alvin Gouldner, "Cosmopolitans and Locals," *Administrative Science Quarterly*, 2 (December 1957; March 1958), 281–306; 444–80. The cosmopolitan-local types focus on a career commitment for which most college professors have well-thought-out, highly articulate notions.

From that context, the present study of the city manager's policy role and behavior evolved.

The principal method used here is the interview survey. The decision to use survey data was set in large measure by the focus on policy expectations and behavior. The only tolerable choice in terms of time and resources was to question city managers and city councilmen themselves. Three major research forays provide most of the reported results: interviews with city managers, mailed questionnaires to city managers, and interviews and questionnaires with city councilmen. In the summer of 1964, forty interviews were conducted with city managers in Alameda, Contra Costa, Marin, San Mateo, and Santa Clara counties.[16] A sample, stratified by city population, was taken, selecting forty out of a possible fifty-three managers.[17] In conducting the interviews, this writer had no refusals and had to make a second visit only once. Working from the same schedule, the length of the interviews ranged from 45 to 180 minutes, with the average about 75. Cooperation was excellent; city managers were articulate and intelligent respondents who seemed to enjoy the chance to voice opinions, judgments, and, quite frequently, complaints.

Second, in the winter of 1965, mail questionnaires were sent to all managers in the Bay Area.[18] (This time the Bay Region was expanded to include Napa, Solano, and Sonoma counties.) Again cooperation was excellent—87 percent (59 out of 68) of the managers took time from busy schedules to complete the questionnaire. Unless otherwise indicated, most of the reported results use data aggregated from these questionnaires. The ques-

---

[16]See Appendix A for field interview schedule.

[17]For economy purposes, a stratified sample of Bay Area cities with ICMA approved managers was taken, selecting forty out of a possible fifty-three. The cities were ordered on the basis of 1960 population. Employing five population categories (1–10,000, 10,000–20,000, 20,000–50,000, 50,000–100,000, 100,000 plus), the cities within each category were ranked by population. With a ratio of forty to fifty-three the appropriate quota of cities from each category was determined. Every other city was then selected, starting from the top. This procedure was repeated until each category quota was filled. In two cases, alternate cities had to be substituted. In Walnut Creek, the city manager quit to become a director in Bay Area Rapid Transit. Livermore was then chosen. And the city manager of Belvedere retired before he could be interviewed. Sausalito was selected as the replacement.

[18]See Appendix B for a copy of questionnaire.

tionnaire itself was developed from the experience with the field interviews.

The third and final source of data is the City Council Research Project. The Project has collected interview and questionnaire data from over three hundred and fifty city councilmen in the San Francisco Bay Area (including the counties of Alameda, Contra Costa, Marin, Napa, San Mateo, Santa Clara, Solano, and Sonoma).[19] The responses to selected questions are used to examine policy expectations of city councilmen for city managers, and to a lesser extent for themselves and the policy process. The selected questions in the Project interview and questionnaire schedules were included and designed to obtain relevant and comparable data from city councilmen.

Bay Area City Managers

California is the "happy hunting ground" for city managers.[20] The state has approximately 280 managers, 100 more than its nearest rival, Texas. Moreover, California is the only major state where a majority of its cities have adopted the city manager plan. And in 240 cities of over 5,000 in population, 218 (or 91%) have by charter or ordinance enacted the city manager plan. Specifically, in the San Francisco Bay Area, the plan or its equivalent has been adopted by every major city except for the city of San Francisco.[21]

---

[19] See Appendix D for a discussion of interview and questionnaire procedures and results.

[20] See John Bollens, *Appointed Executive in Local Government: The California Experience* (Los Angeles: Haynes Foundation, 1952), for a comprehensive, though somewhat dated, discussion of city managers in California.

[21] In the San Francisco Bay Area, the popularity of the city manager plan is uncontested. Adoption is not significantly determined by the social, economic, or political characteristics of its cites. Instead, every city over five thousand except two–San Francisco and Pinole–has a "centralized managed" form of government. Five other characteristics of Bay Area cities are also noteworthy. First, they have a wide range of legal authority. "While no objective standard," writes Eugene Lee, "has been developed to measure the degree of a state's home rule, California cities probably enjoy the greatest municipal independence in the country." Eugene Lee, *Politics of Nonpartisanship* (Berkeley and Los Angeles: University of California Press, 1960), p. 13. The broad grant of powers

Beyond adoption measures, many scholars and practitioners remarked that California has assumed a position of innovation and leadership in the city manager field. City manager posts are in heavy demand; professional goals and programs are well accepted. Another major feature is the highly respected League of California Cities which acts as a clearing, communicating, and coordinating center for city managers. Among other things, the League sponsors an annual state-wide manager convention, hosts semiannual conferences in northern and southern California, and encourages frequent county meetings.

Therefore, before the findings from this study can be extrapolated to other city managers in the United States, major differences, if any, between Bay Area and other city managers should be identified. Table 3–1 compares the average city manager in the United States on five characteristics with the average city manager interviewed for this study in 1964. The results underscore important characteristics of Bay Area city managers. They are more likely to have a college education, a social science major, an advanced degree, a higher salary, and an appointment in a larger city than the average city manager in the United States. These composite characteristics illustrate the credentials of a well-trained, professional executive.[22]

---

given by the state to local governments is true for both charter and general law cities. Second, it is rather easy to incorporate a city in California. Cities are thus often incorporated to meet very particularistic purposes. Third, by state law, every elective office is officially nonpartisan. This converges with the national pattern where over 85 percent of the council-manager cities conduct nonpartisan elections. Fourth, in 1965 all Bay Area cities except two elected councilmen-at-large. On the national level, this is true for about 78 percent of the council-manager cities. And, fifth, in about half the council-manager cities in the United States, the mayor is directly elected by the people. At the time of the study, only four Bay Area cities directly elected their mayor.
[22]Though the observation can be overstated, Bay Area managers, especially in terms of education, would appear to be a window to the future directions of the city manager profession. For, as spokesmen for the profession point out, the complex nature of the urban environment will increasingly require a highly trained, socially aware, and politically astute city manager. These points can readily be found in almost every major article on city managers in the municipal journals; good examples are John Pfiffner, "The Job of the City Manager," *Public Management*, 43 (June 1961), 122–25, and Leonard Goodall, "Politics Meets the Urban Executive," *Public Management*, 48 (December 1966), 343–47.

Table 3–1
Profile of the "Average City Manager"
in the United States and in the Bay Area*

Characteristics	United States	Bay Area
Age		
Average	45	44.5
Under 40	34%	30%
Over 60	12%	7%
Level of Education		
College graduate	64%	90%
Advanced degree	23%	52%
Major Course Work		
Social Science	53%	70%
Engineering	32%	15%
Salary		
More than $10,000	56%	100%
More than $15,000	16%	50%
More than $20,000	5%	22%
Size of City		
Average (pop.)	10,000	36,000

*Data on the average city manager in the United States are from David Arnold, "A Profile of City Managers," *Public Management*, 46 (March 1964), 56–60.

Chapter 4

Policy Role: Views of City Managers

"Order must be discovered," says philosopher Jacob Bronowski, "and in a deep sense it must be created."[1] In the drama of politics, political executives are central participants. Yet why these executives do what, when, and how summons forth many, often inconclusive, answers. One approach is to focus on role expectations associated with the political position. These expectations are assumed to provide the executive with a set of norms and meanings to adjust and guide his behavior.

By the activities assigned to his position, the city manager finds himself inextricably involved in the policy process. And we assume that how the manager participates should result in part from his interpretation of the policy role. The primary objective of this chapter is to examine four related questions: How do city managers define their policy role? What differences in definition exist among city managers? How can these differences be explained? And what policy goals and values do city managers stress?

Characteristics of Policy Role

Background of Managers

In contrast to most political executives, city managers have clearly formulated and commonly shared conceptions of the

---

[1]Jacob Bronowski, *Science and Human Values* (New York: Harper & Row, 1956), p. 24.

policy role. The unusual clarity in role definition can be explained by the numerous occasions when the city manager must directly face questions on the policy role. The city manager can read the formal, often detailed specification of his duties and powers in the city's charter or enabling ordinances. He must make decisions on problems that affect the community in important ways, and thus cannot avoid asking "ought" questions about policy activities. But, most important, because of the long-standing and contentious controversy over proper policy activities of the city manager, the manager will frequently discuss and examine the policy role in graduate school, conferences, municipal literature, and even council sessions. The result is that most city managers have self-consciously formulated what their policy role should be.

The general consensus on the content of the policy role proceeds from three special circumstances. To begin, city managers see themselves as members of a profession. The implications of being a professional are suggested by Edward Banfield and James Q. Wilson:

> Whether or not he regards managing cities as his life's work, he knows that it is a profession and that what is "right" or "wrong" both for him and the council is to be found in the professional Code of Ethics and in the "common law" that has grown up around it.[2]

Another result of membership in the city manager profession lies in the exposure to new ideas, programs, and techniques. Such exposure occurs through print and through face-to-face contact at meetings, conferences, or conventions. The International City Managers' Association, for instance, holds national conferences, publishes a monthly journal as well as a variety of handbooks, offers training courses, supplies technical advice or materials, and reports on new municipal developments. And, in California, the League of California Cities acts as a clearing-house for city managers. The League sponsors state conferences, promotes county meetings, publishes assorted reports, and in general, serves as

---

[2]Edward Banfield and James Q. Wilson, *City Politics* (Cambridge, Mass.: Harvard University Press, 1963), p. 174.

a resource center for city managers. These professional activities tend to lessen the parochialism of city managers and provide them with a set of general norms to guide public policy making.

Second, though not prescribed by a legally sanctioned professional education or apprenticeship, a set of common recruitment and socialization patterns characterize the modal city manager. Furthermore, all evidence indicates that these patterns are becoming increasingly important criteria in city manager appointments.[3]

City managers tend to be college educated, usually with an undergraduate major in the social sciences—the most popular being political science. Especially the younger managers have begun or completed master's degrees in public administration. For example, a manager in his early thirties gave this response, "While I was at University of California, I had intended to go to law school. For my undergraduate major in political science, I picked public administration as an option. During my senior year, I became acquainted with Howard Gardner of the League of California Cities. I took a seminar from him and decided that this was the field for me. Upon graduation, I did a year of graduate work at UC in public administration." And it is at graduate school where city managers are exposed to professional concepts, emphases, and values. Two other career patterns foster similar policy role interpretations among city managers. One is that most city managers are appointed from outside the city staff. And when appointed, they usually have had previous city management experience. Because most city councils review many applicants before hiring a manager, these professional credentials of mobility and experience loom as important. It should also be added that the high turnover rate—average tenure in a city is less than five years—reduces localism and further encourages a professional policy ideology. These career choices and experiences serve to fashion a set of general norms to guide participation in the public policy process. (See Table 4–1.)

The third reason is that the city manager as a policy actor has been the subject of continuous exhortation. The two most im-

---

[3]See, for example, *Directory of City Managers 1964* (Chicago: International City Managers' Association, 1964), pp. 6–19.

Table 4–1
Key Career Choices and Experiences
of San Francisco Bay Area City Managers

Career Patterns	Percentage of City Managers (N = 59)
College Education (BA completed)	78
Social Science Major	58
Graduate Work (MA or Law School)	44
Outside Appointment (Not on City Staff)	77
Apprenticeship in City Management (Assistant City Manager, Administrative Assistant, City Manager, etc.)	68

portant sources are the International City Managers' Association and the municipal journals. The ICMA, parent body of the city management profession, circulates good government memoranda and pamphlets. Probably, though, the most conspicuous and influential exhorters are the municipal magazines: *American City, Mayor and Manager, National Civic Review, Public Management, Western City.* These magazines repeatedly tell the city manager how he can or should be a more active and effective policy maker. Content analysis would reveal almost unanimous agreement that the city manager should be a policy innovator and leader. As an innovator, the emphasis is on new programs, policies, or problems. And as a leader, the focus is on the manager as an agent of change, a professional activist responsible for making what Philip Selznick calls critical decisions.[4]

Valuable Tool for Study

The policy role conception of the city manager should be an especially valuable analytical tool to understanding his policy behavior. If role conceptions are stable points of reference, the more clearly defined and central the role expectations, the greater their probable impact on behavior. The city manager's policy role is well defined and capable of being articulated. And it

---

[4]See Philip Selznick, *Leadership in Administration* (New York: Harper & Row, 1957), pp. 29–64.

covers—and in a sense defines—one of the main tasks faced by every city manager: making decisions on problems that commit the city government. Therefore, the policy role refers to important expectations that are personally relevant and functionally significant.

Policy Role Views

There is no one right way to study the policy role conceptions of city managers. We could, for example, develop complex scales of specific expectations culled from municipal journals. Or we could ask city managers their positions on a wide range of community problems from zoning to sewage disposal to off-street parking or racial discrimination. However, most studies by social scientists conclude that policy activities—initiation, formulation, and presentation of policy proposals—primarily involve intangibles such as consultation, discussion, advising, and the informal bringing together of information and data, and that successes are largely determined by the demands of the immediate situation. Rather than identify specific expectations, this study attempts to distinguish general policy commitments, or put differently, "styles" of policy making. Thus, the focus becomes one of how the city manager believes he should participate in terms of major innovation and leadership objectives.

To identify policy role views, city managers were asked nine questions. These questions were designed to discover the direction and content of the role conceptions of the city manager. We asked: "Now ever since the council-manager plan was first adopted, there has been much disagreement over what a city manager should or should not do. Here are nine questions on the job of being a city manager. Read each question and then decide which one of the four answers most closely describes how you feel—do you strongly agree, tend to agree, tend to disagree, or strongly disagree?"[5] (See Table 4–2.)

---

[5]The policy expectation items were devised and selected from an evaluation of the study's objectives and after a review of the city manager literature—in particular, some questions were drawn from Jeptha Carrell, *Role of the City Manager* (Kansas City, Mo.: Community Studies, 1962).

Table 4–2
City Manager Policy Role Views

	Percentages	
Questions	Agree	Disagree
1. *Policy Innovator*—A city manager should assume leadership in shaping municipal policies. (N = 57)	88	12
2. *Policy Advocate*—A city manager should advocate major changes in city policies. (N = 58)	81	19
3. *Policy Administrator*—A city manager should act as an administrator and leave policy matters to the council. (N = 58)	22	78
4. *Policy Neutral*—A city manager should maintain a neutral stand on any issues on which the community is divided. (N = 58)	24	76
5. *Budget Consultant*—A city manager should consult with the council before drafting his own budget. (N = 58)	31	69
6. *Political Advocate*—A city manager should advocate policies to which important parts of the community may be hostile. (N = 58)	55	45
7. *Political Leader*—A city manager should work through the most powerful members of the community to achieve policy goals. (N = 58)	53	47
8. *Political Recruiter*—A city manager should encourage people whom he respects to run for city council. (N = 57)	44	56
9. *Political Campaigner*—A city manager should give a helping hand to good councilmen who are coming up for reelection. (N = 59)	25	75

City manager agreement is striking on most major policy expectations. While some differences exist, most city managers see themselves as active participants in the policy process. To be specific (see items 1–5), there is overwhelming agreement that the city manager should be a policy innovator and policy advocate. Such participation is viewed as much more than a staff service of information gathering; as two managers explain:

> A city manager is obligated to bring his expertise, experience, and ability to the council. He should actively take part in policy recommendations. Common sense would indicate that a full time manager trained and experienced in municipal affairs should make recommendations to what is essentially an amateur, part time council.

> I feel the city manager is like the general manager for a large corporation. He has to administer the city. But more than that, he should set forth strong recommendations to his council on all matters of policy which have to do with the welfare of the city. And he should attempt to sell diligently his recommendations.

Three out of four managers reject the classic administration-politics dichotomy that assigns the manager only administrative responsibilities. Managers think they should be involved in the resolution of controversial issues, in the taking of policy positions rather than retiring behind the cloak of professional neutrality.

Somewhat less agreement is evinced on more politicized and community related activities (see items 6–8). On matters of community conflict, some city managers are reluctant to act as policy advocates; nevertheless, over half believe they should take policy positions even in the face of important opposition in the community.

And beyond advocating policies, a majority of managers think a city manager should work directly with influential members of the community to achieve policy goals. These results point to the self-conception of many managers as political leaders and not simply as municipal executors for the community power structure.

Perhaps the best measure of the strong policy role expressed by many managers is the normative expectation among 40 percent of the managers that they should "encourage people . . . to run for city council." Some twenty-five out of fifty-eight respondents believe a proper function of the city manager is to influence the cast of legislators. But, finally, there is general agreement on one prohibition: a city manager should not get involved in the political campaigns of city councilmen—though a number of city managers privately indicated that they have written speeches and planned strategies for incumbent councilmen. Yet, as a whole, the one political activity most managers believe they should avoid is electioneering. Beyond this professional taboo, the city manager has few normative restrictions on the breadth or style of his involvement in the public policy process. A composite self-image emerges of a strong political executive, expected to exert policy leadership on most demands or issues before the city agenda.

Policy Role Orientations

Although there is much agreement among managers as to what they should do in the policy process, they nonetheless differ in the definition of their policy role. They entertain different normative views regarding their place in policy making, some being more willing to innovate and assume leadership than others. These differences deserve inquiry in their own right; for we can construct out of them a general typology of role orientations.[6]

City manager scores on the nine questions found in Table 4–2 yield a major policy role typology. For the response scores of the managers demonstrate patterned differences in how the policy role is defined. Each manager can be placed on a continuum in terms of the direction and strength of his commitment to participate in the policy process. These patterned differences in policy role conceptions will be typed as Political and Administrative orientations. On occasion, each major policy orientation will be subdivided into Political Leader and Political Executive types and Administrative Director and Administrative Technician types. Here the purpose is to use more refined categories to spotlight trends and more subtle distinctions. (A careful account of the rules and procedures for the typology can be found in

---

[6]See Neal Gross, Ward Mason, and Alexander McEachern, *Explorations in Role Analysis* (New York: John Wiley & Sons, 1958), pp. 319–27. They conclude, "Our research suggests that different expectations held for incumbents' behavior and attributes are crucial for an understanding of their different behaviors and characteristics" (p. 231).

Appendix C.) When responses of Bay Area managers were scored and typed, the distribution was as follows:

Policy Orientations		Number of Managers
Political		30
	Political Leader 12	
	Political Executive 18	
	——	
	30	
Administrative		28
	Administrative Director 16	
	Administrative Technician 12	
	——	
	28	

   The claim that Political and Administrative orientations represent two relatively distinct approaches to policy making requires explication of the major differences that exist. To begin, the average responses of the four types on each closed question point to important role differences (Table 4–3).[7] Political types believe the manager should innovate and lead on policy matters. Further, they endorse direct participation on issues of community conflict and controversy, drawing back only on the question of political campaigning for city councilmen. In contrast, Administrative types take a much more limited view of the manager's policy role. Ambivalent about innovation and leadership on policy matters, these managers readily reject involvement in community politics. Administrative managers prefer, in short, a neutral definition of the policy role in which the city manager acts more like a staff adviser than a political executive.

   Interview responses also distinguish policy role differences. Grouped by policy types, the interview results were carefully

---

[7]Admittedly the relationships are exaggerated because the policy orientations are derived from the closed questions. However, the purpose is to contrast rather than to prove differences in policy role views.

Table 4–3
Average Responses of Policy Role Types
to the Nine Closed Questions

	AVERAGE RESPONSES OF POLICY TYPES*			
	Political		*Administrative*	
Questions	Leader (N=12)	Executive (N=18)	Director (N=16)	Technician (N=12)
	$\overline{X}$	$\overline{X}$	$\overline{X}$	$\overline{X}$
1. Policy Innovator	+2.9	+1.7	+1.0	0.0
2. Policy Advocate	+2.7	+1.7	+1.1	−0.7
3. Policy Administrator	−2.2	−1.1	+0.6	+0.7
4. Policy Neutral	−1.5	−1.1	−0.7	+0.2
5. Budget Consultant	−1.5	−1.4	−0.9	−0.3
6. Political Advocate	+1.3	+0.5	−0.4	−0.8
7. Political Leader	+1.2	+0.6	−0.3	−0.5
8. Political Recruiter	+1.3	+0.1	−0.8	−2.3
9. Political Campaigner	−0.6	−1.4	−1.3	−1.8

*Manager responses were translated into numerical scores as follows:
strongly agree = +3; tend to agree = +1; tend to disagree = −1; and strongly disagree = −3.

studied. Major attention was given to one question: "Now, ever since the council-manager plan was first adopted, there has been much disagreement over what a city manager should or should not do. How would you describe the job of a city manager—what are the most important things you should or should not do?" Responses to this question will illustrate how the manager types interpret the policy role. And perhaps it should be noted that the remarks which follow, excepting quotations, are a general interpretation of the interview responses of managers from each policy type.[8]

Political Leaders take the broadest view of the policy role, giving enthusiastic endorsement to managers as idea men and agents of change. Great emphasis is placed on problems and pro-

[8]Whenever city managers are directly quoted, data are from field interviews conducted in the summer of 1964. In each instance, city managers were also typed by the same procedures used for the questionnaire responses.

grams as well as the manager's obligation to act as an advocate of policy and a political leader. These managers espouse a political readiness to act as plaintiffs for good government and the public interest. The responses of two managers highlight the Political Leader orientation:

> the most important things are to bring to the attention of the city council the problems and needs of the community, to propose solutions to these problems, to keep the council informed on city operations, and to provide effective leadership for the administrative staff. . . . A city manager is obligated to bring his expertise, experience, and ability to the council. He should actively take part in policy recommendations. Common sense would indicate that a full time manager trained and experienced in municipal affairs should make recommendations to what is essentially an amateur, part time council. If a decision affects the town, a city manager has the responsibility to get involved. For a city manager has a responsibility to the community as well as to the council. A city manager should pursue certain political objectives, although perhaps not openly.

> Well . . . first, a city manager should administratively control and operate the city. This is the way it is locally judged. He should have complete administrative authority, for example, to make personnel changes. . . . Second, a city manager must be involved in the policy making area. Council establishes policy; however, a city manager should be involved in what kind of policy it is. Both the city manager and the council should be involved as equals in preliminary discussions; the council then makes the final decisions. . . . The city manager has to be a planner in the best sense of the word. He should be a supervisor—rather, he has to be a planner . . . he also has to be a leader.

Political Executives share many of the same policy goals and approaches as Political Leaders, for they too believe a manager should be an innovator and leader. The major difference is one of degree rather than kind. Though holding broad views of the policy role, their policy style is tempered by such factors as personal experience or political environment. The Political Executive is less willing to stick his neck out, whether to recruit councilmen or to push major policies, and he takes a more pragmatic and less moralistic view of the political role of the manager. To illustrate, two managers ably express the orientation patterns of a Political Executive:

> The real distinction is what you should not do publicly in contrast to what you must do privately. A city manager should be more than a council adviser. He should urge and recommend policy. He should write policies for others to present. Of course, a city manager's activity depends on the caliber of the council. Especially if it is poor, the city manager should lead from behind the scenes. But he should not lead publicly. This can be the kiss of death. You have to be careful. I think a city manager should be a faceless man in the community. . . . All credit should go to the council. If a city manager accepts credit, then he must also accept blame.
>
> The manager to resolve community problems has to determine how he can get in step with the community, not how the community can get in step with him. . . . A city manager has got to have a sense of timing. For he can win battles but lose the war. If a city manager pushes too many programs at once—although they may be needed—he can become a divisive influence. If he uses common sense, he can find out what the council and community would support. By weighing support for programs, progress might take more time but the results will be better.

Administrative Directors share an ambivalence, combining a professional yet local commitment to policy making. Generally convinced that managers should actively participate in the policy process, Administrative Directors nevertheless articulate a reluctance to be novel innovators or open leaders. Instead, they tend to be preoccupied with the art of the possible, stressing constraints rather than problems, the council's authority as opposed to the manager's expertise. Though recognizing the imperative of a manager assuming an active role, the conception is typically more negative than positive: "The city manager, whether he likes it or not, gets involved in policy questions." Two managers suggest the tension between activism and restraint held by Administrative Directors:

> Essentially the city manager is employed to carry out the policies of the representatives of the people, the governing body. This is the most important point. I should do the job in accord with the council's decisions and directions. In serving in this role, the city

manager can work with and effect decisions of the council. He does this through studies and recommendations. Thus the city manager substantially influences the course of government. I do not see a city manager as the leader of the community. It seems to me that he should be in the background and work through the council. It is best if the council carries the ball.

A city manager should involve himself with the direction of the administrative activities of the city to the best of his abilities. . . . I do not think a city manager should engage in political activities, in pressuring the council, or in supporting particular interests in the community. It is inevitable that a city manager becomes involved in policy making. There is no escape. . . . While a city manager becomes involved, he should not do so openly but by employing tact and diplomacy. He has to be concerned with issues that affect the operations of the city; he cannot remain silent.

Finally, Administrative Technicians define the policy role within a narrow context, closely resembling the classic dichotomy between politics and administration. The focus is on administrative decisions or what managers call housekeeping functions. Rather than propose change, Administrators see themselves as handmaidens of the status quo or as curators of established goals. As to policy leadership, Administrators view themselves as staff advisers, clearly subordinate to the councils. Three managers suggest these twin features of the Administrative Technicians' perspective:

The most important things are: Policy decisions to the council, administrative decisions to the city manager. Just that simple. Of course, there are grey areas; here there must be some kind of agreement—a method of exchanging information.

A city manager should act as the chief administrative officer of the city BUT under the direction of the council. And he should be the staff adviser to the council on the development of policy. Those are the most important things.

Four things—first, a city manager should carry out—and this is most important—the policy of the city council. Second, a city manager has an obligation to provide the council with sound recommendations and policies. Third, a city manager should provide the council with the best technical information available. And, fourth, a city manager has the responsibility not to take over the council's political and policy role.

Sources of Policy Orientations

Role conceptions are complex, interrelated products of personal, social, and cultural experiences. In asking antecedent questions, one is thus faced with almost insoluble dilemmas. The choice will be an eclectic approach focused on two kinds of variables—personal and community. Can the policy role differences be accounted for by personal background, community conditions, a combination of these, or what? Needless to say, the hope is to choose and explore variables that appear to be promising explanatory sources of policy role differences.

Personal Characteristics

The explanatory emphasis for role conceptions has centered on demands lodged in the social structure and particularly the expectations of so-called significant others. Yet role views are, in large measure, the product of personal definition. As Alex Inkeles points out:

> Without in any way challenging the crucial importance of the objective factors which determine role behavior, I wish to stress that recruitment into roles and the quality of role performance may to an important degree be influenced by personal qualities in individuals which predispose them to move toward one or another role, and which have a marked effect on the quality of their role performance once they have been placed. It must be assumed, further, that this happens on a sufficiently large scale to be a crucial factor in determining the functioning of any social system.[9]

There is good reason to expect that personal characteristics importantly contribute to the development and adoption of differing policy role orientations by city managers.

---

[9]Alex Inkeles, "Personality and Social Structure," in *Sociology Today,* Robert Merton, Leonard Broom, and Leonard Cottrell, eds. (New York: Harper & Row, 1959), p. 267.

Career Circumstances. The city manager moves through a sequence of career choices and patterns that should influence his
policy views, for these career experiences inexorably link the
past with the present. Among city managers, these experiences
can differ importantly; in point of fact, these differences provide
a major focus for analysis (Table 4–4).

Administrative and Political managers differ strikingly in terms
of educational experiences. Administrative types reveal varied
educational backgrounds. In contrast, Political types share the
educational credentials endorsed by the city management profession—a college diploma with a major in the social sciences
followed by graduate work in public administration. Especially
at graduate school, a would-be manager is likely to develop a
broad and forceful view of the policy role, for here he is exposed
to the problems of the public interest and public welfare, the
need for planning and leadership, and shibboleths like the administration-politics dichotomy. In effect, these schools should
act as politicizing agents. Certainly the two most prominent West
Coast graduate schools, the University of California at Berkeley
and the University of Southern California, are strong and long-
time advocates of the philosophy that the urban manager should
be a major policy innovator and community leader.

Closely related to educational background is the choice of an
occupation, perhaps the most crucial decision an individual
makes in his lifetime. In the field interviews, city managers were
asked, "Why did you go into city management?" Abridged life
histories varied widely in substance and focus; yet two distinct
occupational choice patterns were clearly evident. One is an
accidental choice, a choice centered on an unexpected web of
circumstances—for example, "My initial background was in law.
In effect, I became a city manager as a result of an illness. I was
legal officer in a town in Ohio and when the city manager became
sick, I was appointed to take his place, first on a temporary basis,
then permanently." Conversely, the second pattern is a *planned
choice.* Some managers self-consciously decide to enter city management at the university level—for example, "As an undergraduate, I majored in history and government. Upon graduation, I

Career Choices and Patterns	POLITICAL		ADMINISTRATIVE	
	Political		*Administrative*	
	Leader (N=12)	Executive (N=18)	Director (N=16)	Technician (N=12)
College Education (BA completed)	92%	94%	69%	42%
Social Science Major	67%	61%	44%	8%
Graduate Work (MA or Law School)	67%	89%	38%	33%
Outside Appointment (Not on City Staff)	75%	94%	63%	67%
Apprenticeship in City Management	75%	78%	44%	58%
Years in Municipal Government, 15 or less	83%	56%	63%	33%

went to Michigan State and received an M.A. in political science, specializing in local government."

With noteworthy exceptions, accidental choices are made by Administrative managers and planned choices by Political managers. These two patterns of career choice are important because they often indicate major differences in value commitments. The emphasis of managers expressing accidental choices tends to focus on opportunities for personal reward or advancement. To illustrate, one Administrative manager offered this short biography:

> After graduating with a B.S., I worked for the California Water Service as a civil engineer for nine years. When I saw I had more or less reached a plateau in my job, I looked for a position where greater opportunity for advancement could be found. I became Water Superintendent, then was appointed Director of Public Works and Utilities. In February, 1962, I was named city manager.

In contrast, the rationale for planned choices tends to center on some statement of public service.

Another recruitment pattern presents a possible crucible for policy role differences. Early proponents of the city manager plan sought to have selection based on the best man for the position. At the minimum, this implied hiring from outside the city, and especially outside the city staff, for such procedures were thought necessary if the city manager was to be a professional and divorced from local interests. In point of fact, appointments are now highly competitive, with most councils reviewing long lists of candidates. Nonetheless, it is noteworthy that twelve out of the sixteen managers promoted or co-opted from the city staff hold Administrative orientations. These locals are usually novice managers, probably appointed because their policy style and values converge with those of the council.

If the city manager develops his policy views in the course of professional apprenticeship, two other career patterns deserve attention. First, Political managers are more likely than Administrative managers to have served an apprenticeship in city management. Most Political managers and some Administrative managers follow the career ladder from assistant city manager to city manager. Beginning with high hopes for a career in city management, these managers should be readily socialized into the goals and objectives of the profession. However, less than half of the Administrative managers have served in management apprenticeships. Instead, they have been appointed from such offices as city engineer, finance director, public works director, personnel director, building inspector, tax inspector, and even mayor. And, second, participation in the governmental game ranges from a few years to over forty. Time played seems to make some difference for managers with the strongest policy role views. Political Leaders tend to be newcomers to city government, with policy views untempered by personal fatigue or political battles. On the other hand, Administrative Technicians have been participants in the governmental game for a long time and, as a result, are much less enthusiastic and optimistic about the costs of involvement and the prospects for change. Differences in years of municipal service reveal a kind of generation gap between the young comers and old guard of city management. Yet, for whatever reasons, wide differences exist in years of municipal service between Political Leaders and Administrative Technicians.[10]

Reference Groups. The search for personal explanations of policy orientation should include reference groups. Sociologist Robert Merton writes that reference group theory deals with "the determinants and consequences of those processes of evaluation and self-appraisal in which the individual takes the values or standards of other individuals and groups as comparative frames of reference."[11] A reference group is a group whose presumed perspective is used by a city manager as a frame of reference in the organization of his policy views. The major hypothesis implicit in the literature on local government is that the greater the professional identification, the broader the manager's policy conception.

To identify the groups that a city manager considers important to his reputation, the question was asked:

> A city manager's reputation is said to depend on the approval of a number of different publics. Some publics, however, are probably more important than others. How would you rank the following on their importance to your reputation as a city manager?
>
> Administrative Staff_____   Council_____
> Fellow City Managers_____   Community Groups_____
> Public-at-Large_____   Professional Management Groups_____

Notable agreement exists among city managers on the relative importance of each group. The overall choices were the same for the four policy types: (1) council; (2) staff; (3) community groups;

---

[10]In addition to differences in career stages, another promising explanation for the apparent relationship between years of service and policy orientations could lie in the historical influence of various periods on recruitment and training. That is, as the job of the city manager evolved from city hall's chief engineer to its chief executive, so too should these changes be reflected in the reasons for entering city management and the training in the major graduate programs. In other words, years of service may not be as important as the period of entry and training in city management.

[11]Robert Merton, *Social Theory and Social Structure* (rev. ed.; Glencoe, Ill.: The Free Press, 1957), p. 234.

(4) public-at-large; (5) fellow city managers; and (6) professional management groups. The results point to near unanimity on what groups are thought to be important contributors to a manager's general reputation. However, besides indicating that almost every manager opts first for council rather than colleague approval, little evidence is offered on the question initially posed: does professional identification influence a city manager's policy conception?

Also, when asked to comment on identification with the profession, managers expressed important differences; for approval and allegiance to city management varied noticeably from Political Leaders to Administrative Technicians. To illustrate, generally typical responses of the four policy types can be found below:

> POLITICAL LEADER: Well. . . . I am proud to be a member. And at the same time, I am filled with a deep feeling of the awesome responsibility. I have a responsibility to aid the profession, to build a good public image of the city manager. I have an individual responsibility in my own community to be an asset in helping the community achieve its potential. I go to national ICMA conferences regularly. I am impressed with the ICMA's recognition of its professional responsibility. I mean by this its help, for example, in researching the individual needs of city managers. In the eight years I have been in the field, the role of the city manager has changed. The council-manager form is much more accepted, the tenure of the city manager is greater, and the education requirements have increased.

> POLITICAL EXECUTIVE: Let's stop and think. Most city managers are not academically trained to be managers. They do not have MA's in public administration. I do not think we have achieved the level of a true profession, although we are going in that direction. Personally, I am proud to be able to work in this field. Proud is too self-serving. Appreciative is a better word. I look to the day when I will be a member of a professional group—even if this includes registration. Effectiveness is the real measure of a manager. How well can he improve and implement council and community policies. This has to be judged over a long period of time.

> ADMINISTRATIVE DIRECTOR: I have no strong feelings about the profession. I am interested in public affairs. I would consider work-

ing in other public areas, e.g., for the state, for a Congressman. I feel there is nothing magical about a city manager or city administrator. On the other hand, I don't mean to say that this is not a worthwhile profession. The city managers are of great value to the country and state. They have important influences on the social and economic problems at the local level. Of course, how much a city manager can influence public policy depends on the power and prestige of the individual city manager.

ADMINISTRATIVE TECHNICIAN: Calling city managers a profession is like calling construction an industry. To be a city manager, you need a certain amount of experience, a certain amount of savvy. There are no particular courses which you take in school to make you a city manager. A city manager is not a professional in any sense of the word.

These interview responses indicate why professional identification could partially influence the manager's policy role views. Professional success in terms of mobility or status is predicated on concrete achievements or, as one study reported, "doing things to move to more desirable cities." Commitment to the profession as a reference group should thus influence what a city manager thinks he should or should not do as a policy maker.

Perhaps the most satisfactory measure of professional identification is professional activity. The problem, however, becomes one of selection. Attendance at national ICMA conferences is a dubious indicator because some managers do not have the option of going. Membership in the ICMA is also unsatisfactory, for most managers are ICMA members. The kind or number of municipal periodicals received also fails to discriminate: little manager discretion is involved—some are sent free, others are subscribed to by most cities. After rejecting these possibilities and several other measures, attendance at conferences sponsored by the League of California Cities was selected as the criterion (Table 4–5). Here almost all city managers have the chance to go or stay at home. Political managers, with few exceptions, attend all or most League meetings. On the other hand, almost half of the Administrative managers report infrequent attendance at League meetings. While not true for all Administrative managers, low attendance clearly seems a characteristic of managers with Administrative

Table 4–5
Relation of Attendance at League Conferences
to Policy Role Types*

| | POLICY TYPES | | | |
| | Political | | Administrative | |
Attendance	Leader (N = 12)	Executive (N = 17)	Director (N = 16)	Technician (N = 12)
High	92%	82%	56%	50%
Low	8%	18%	44%	50%

*City managers were asked: "Do you attend all, most, some, few, or none of the city manager conferences sponsored by the League of California Cities?" Categories "all" and "most" were coded as high attendance and "some," "few," and "none" as low attendance.

orientations. It is at conferences that managers intermingle socially, discuss common problems, find out what is going on in other cities, and so forth. Conference activity should thus be one measure of professional identification. If so, the hypothesis that the greater the professional identification, the more likely it is that a manager will hold strong policy views finds some support in the available data on Bay Area managers.

Political Philosophy. When a narrow versus a broad interpretation of the policy role is discussed, political ideology in the form of conservatism and liberalism is a common explanation. A conservative stance is viewed as a limited conception of the role of government, while a liberal position suggests a wider conception of government's duties and responsibilities. Differences, therefore, focus on the extent of government activity: To what degree should the government assume interest, responsibility, and control over various sectors of the social and economic order? An important corollary is posture toward change. Conservatives are seen as reluctant to change the existing order in contrast to liberals who supposedly favor continual improvement and purposeful change.[12] The argument would thus read that the more

---

[12]For a short, clear discussion of conservatism-liberalism as an ideological posture, see Angus Campbell, Philip Converse, Warren Miller, and Donald Stokes, *The American Voter* (New York: John Wiley & Sons, 1960), pp. 168–215.

politically conservative a manager, the more likely he is to hold an Administrative orientation.

Most city managers prefer to classify themselves as political moderates, with pragmatism as the appropriate response to socio-political questions. In fact, self-perceptions of city managers would seem to deny the existence of any major ideological differences. When asked, "Generally speaking, would you describe yourself as a liberal, moderate, or conservative?" a majority of the managers interviewed found cause to object to the labels or to criticize the question. Rather, they wanted to emphasize a pragmatic rather than doctrinaire approach, for they were unwilling to translate city problem solving into abstract political ideologies.

To secure discrete measures of political ideology, city managers completed a twelve item political-economic conservatism scale.[13] The managers were then rank ordered by scores and divided into three more or less equal groups. Representing the relative direction and intensity of conservative scores, these groups were designated as conservative, moderate, and liberal. Also, to focus on a less inclusive ideological measure, a scope of government index was constructed from three scale questions that have concrete references to so-called proper activities of government:

1) When private enterprise does not do the job well, it is up to the government to step in and meet the public's need for housing, water, power, and the like.

2) The government should own and operate all public utilities (gas, electric, water).

3) The government should develop a program of health insurance and medical care.

Again, the same procedure as above was used to divide the managers into conservative, moderate, and liberal groups (Table 4–6).

Administrative managers tend to hold more limited conceptions of what proper government activities are than do Political managers. These political views could influence how a city man-

---

[13]The political-economic conservatism scale is taken from Gross et al., *Explorations in Role Analysis,* pp. 183–92, 364–65.

Table 4–6
Relation of Policy Orientations
to Conservative–Liberal Scores

Conservative–Liberal Measure	Policy Orientations	
	Political (N = 29)	Administrative (N = 27)
Conservative	24%	41%
Moderate	31%	37%
Liberal	45%	22%
Scope of Government Measure	Political (N = 30)	Administrative (N = 28)
Conservative	23%	46%
Moderate	43%	39%
Liberal	34%	15%

ager will define his approach to policy matters. If a city manager believes that government should be minimized as much as possible, this stance should predispose him toward the role of housekeeper—one Administrative manager, for example, expressed his political outlook as follows:

> I am of the opinion that government generally speaking should be minimized as much as it can be and still promote and preserve the peace, safety, and welfare of the citizens. I too place considerable emphasis on economy in government.

Political beliefs are most critical to policy role definitions when managers hold these beliefs with certainty and intensity. The several managers that the scale identifies as political ideologues have all adopted the expected policy orientation. To illustrate, the manager with the highest liberal score on both measures in Table 4–6 was also the most aggressive and outspoken Political manager. To a question on political philosophy, he replied, "I am an old time radical with an honorable history. I fought strike breakers, marched in picket lines, and so forth: I was a Wobbly!" The manager's political values should, in summary, be included as possible major determinants of policy orientations. Indeed, Administrative managers tend to be associated with a more conservative outlook than Political managers.

Community Characteristics

The city manager thinks and acts within the context of a community. The community presents the city manager with specific conditions—social, economic, and political—that delimit what he can or cannot do as a policy maker. These conditions represent a second possible source for policy orientations. Yet what community characteristics should we examine? There are many kinds of Bay Area cities—old, new; Republican, Democratic; rich, poor; residential, industrial; large, small; upper class, middle class, working class; homogeneous, heterogeneous; central, suburb; and so forth. The assumption is that each of these characteristics confronts the city manager with different clusters of attitudes, values, and interests.

To explore the question of whether community conditions influence the interpretation of the policy role, three community characteristics will be examined: political complexity, political values, and population characteristics. The local government literature suggests these characteristics could be especially promising explanatory conditions for differences in policy role conceptions. In making inferences from community characteristics to policy orientations, an unresolved problem requires comment. Any relationship between community characteristics and policy orientations could as well be explained by the recruitment process as by the influence of the community. City managers are both self-recruited and recruited by city councils. For one, they can be quite selective in applying for and accepting city manager posts. Managers could opt for communities that are compatible with their career ambitions and policy conceptions. Or, second, city councils review a large number of applicants. It is likely that the council would appoint a manager whose policy views are in agreement with the community's attitudes, values, and interests. In other words, the sociopolitical character of each community could tend to recruit managers with either Political or Administrative policy orientations. It is also true, however, that a manager may be chosen for traditional managerial skills, but, once in office, he may become the advocate for policy objectives that were not considered at the time of his appointment. For purposes here, no attempt will be made to identify the causal process by which community characteristics and policy orientations are related. Rather, we will examine what associations exist, if any, between three community characteristics and Political and Administrative orientations, and where relevant, offer interpretations on why such patterns could occur.

Political Complexity. The most obvious characteristic of a community is size of population. City limit signs proclaim the latest population figures. "How large is the city?" is usually the first question asked about a community. Beyond visibility and popular interest, population size is important for the political analyst. Many generalizations can be found on the effect of community size on the political process. Here size is used as a measure of political complexity. It is assumed that the larger the city, the more complex the political process: political stakes should be more bountiful, competing interests more numerous, community consensus more variable, policy making more specialized, policy problems more diverse and intractable, and so forth.

Statements on the relation of the city manager as policy maker to population size are numerous and contradictory. In fact, generalizations run both ways: the smaller the city, the more likely a manager will be a policy activist; or, the larger the city, the more likely a manager will be a policy activist. When cities are divided into three population groups—10,000 or less; 10,000–50,000; and 50,000 or above—one result is conspicuous (Table 4–7). Small cities are much more likely to have managers with Administrative than Political orientations, but no other relationships are apparent for either middle or large cities.

Let us look at one interpretation of why cities with populations below 10,000 might foster a limited conception of the policy role. In small cities, routine problems become the major responsibility of the city manager; thus his activities tend to be those of policy implementation and not policy formulation or political bargain-

Table 4-7
Relation of Community Size to Policy Orientations

| Policy Orientation | Population Groups | | |
	10,000 or less (N = 17)	10,000– 50,000 (N = 32)	50,000 or more (N = 9)
Political	29%	62%	55%
Administrative	71%	38%	45%

ing. When required to center his attention and anxiety on house-keeping functions, the city manager could develop a narrow policy conception. For example, an Administrative manager in a small city whose career characteristics are those of a Political manager—e.g., MA in Public Administration from the University of Southern California—made this lament:

> The extremely heavy workload placed on the city manager here is a perennial frustration. In a small city, you have no staff to delegate work to. And it takes a long time to adopt sound programs— the staff is more often than not overwhelmed with everyday problems. Right now, I have just about got some uniform traffic and subdivision ordinances worked out after four years. . . . I am a paper flunky.

Yet it is equally true that size does not guarantee a broad conception of the policy role; we need, therefore, to look at other community characteristics.

Political Values. Two political scientists, Oliver Williams and Charles Adrian, developed a typology of political values pivoted on the role of government. Cities are classified in terms of four actual policy emphases: (1) promoting economic growth; (2) providing or securing life's amenities; (3) maintaining traditional services; and (4) arbitrating among conflicting interests.[14] After a comparative study of four Michigan cities, Williams and Adrian concluded that the cities oriented toward the policy values of

---

[14]See Oliver Williams and Charles Adrian, *Four Cities* (Philadelphia: University of Pennsylvania Press, 1963), pp. 11–39.

economic growth and amenities will permit and foster a broad or what they called a problem-solving definition of the policy role. And, conversely, caretaker and arbiter oriented cities will discourage and limit such a definition; for these policy emphases set up political circumstances hostile to manager innovation and leadership.[15]

Cities, however, do not fit neatly or readily into any one of the four categories. It is probable that most city governments will have varying commitments to all the political values of the Williams and Adrian typology. Classification thus becomes somewhat arbitrary, focusing on the degree of a city government's commitment. Moreover, the four types of cities do not lend themselves to rigorous measurement; so classification has to be a matter of expert judgment. To type Bay Area cities, city managers were asked the following question:

> Communities are incorporated for different reasons, perform different functions. Here is a list of four kinds of city government. How would you rank the four in the order which they most closely describe your city?
>
> 1. Our city government promotes community growth. We facilitate and encourage commercial and industrial expansion.
>
> 2. Our city government promotes "suburban" living. We provide a high level of community services.
>
> 3. Our city government promotes small government, low taxation. We limit community growth, maintain traditional services.
>
> 4. Our city government is unable to promote any one interest. We work out policies with a number of conflicting interests.

The first choices of city managers point to several important patterns (Table 4-8). The political values of either economic growth or amenities predominate in three out of four Bay Area cities. The results would indicate, according to Williams and Adrian, that these cities should support, if not encourage, a strong professional orientation by the manager. Nevertheless, cities that emphasize economic growth and providing amenities show no major differences in the total number of managers with Political and Administrative orientations. Rather, the political values of economic growth and amenities appear to have little in

[15]*Ibid.*, pp. 150–64.

Table 4–8

Relation of Role of Government to Policy Orientations

| Policy Orientation | Roles of City Government | | | |
	Economic Growth (N = 27)	Amenities (N = 15)	Caretaker (N = 7)	Arbiter (N = 8)
Political	59%	40%	14%	75%
Administrative	41%	60%	86%	25%

the way of a distinctive influence on the policy role orientations of city managers.

On the other hand, caretaker cities have almost exclusively managers with Administrative orientations. And, as Williams and Adrian suggest, caretaker cities require or at least encourage a narrow definition of the policy role. However, for arbiter cities, the pattern is quite the reverse from what is predicted: six out of eight arbiter cities have managers with Political orientations. Rather than inhibiting a broad definition of the policy role, the lack of agreement on political values appears to call for highly politicized managers. Perhaps the arbiter city gives a city manager authority to more directly articulate and work toward executive policy objectives for city government.

Demographic Make-Up. Population characteristics are a third approach to policy role demands. Socioeconomic status is probably the most important of many demographic characteristics; for, as Jones, Forstall, and Collver comment:

> . . . of major importance as a measure of a city's ability to meet and solve its problems, as well as an index of the demands made upon the city, is the composition of the population in terms of socioeconomic status. Political participation and the focus of politics are likely to be different in cities with a high proportion of high-income, white collar, home-owning, white residents than in cities with the opposite characteristics.[16]

[16]Victor Jones, Richard Forstall, and Andrew Collver, "Economic and Social Characteristics of Urban Places," in *Municipal Year Book 1963*, Orin Nolting and David Arnold, eds. (Chicago: International City Managers' Association, 1963), p. 85.

Further, in *Class in Suburbia,* William Dobriner contends that class variables critically define the character of political activities in a community.[17] If these observations are valid, cities with different class characteristics should make different value demands on the city manager. The one generalization most often propounded is a convergence of interests between professional managers and upper middle-class communities, and a state of tension, even overt conflict, between professional managers and working-class communities. To examine such interpretations, the Bay Area cities were rank ordered by median income and then divided into three equal groups (Table 4–9).

Class differences would appear to be related to policy orientations—yet not in the direction first anticipated. Administrative managers are more likely to be found in high-income cities, and Political managers in low-income cities.[18] The results in the Bay Area study suggest that high-income cities could place major policy constraints on what the city manager believes he should do. And cities with lower incomes may encourage if not require the manager to see himself as initiating and seeking important policy changes. Also, the lower the median income of a city, the more likely a city manager will be on a personal status level higher than his councilmen. This circumstance could perhaps lead the manager to develop a forceful and aggressive view of the policy role. But, regardless of the interpretation, a positive

---

17See William Dobriner, *Class in Suburbia* (Englewood Cliffs, N.J.: Prentice-Hall, 1963) , pp. 29–60.

18On a continuum of all United States cities, most of the low-income cities in Table 4–9 would not fall into the lowest third. However, the income level of these cities has to be considered with several factors in mind. First, suburbs differ from central and independent cities. By and large, the income levels of suburbs are higher. Second, suburbs with the city manager plan differ from those with the mayor or commission form. Again, the income levels tend to be higher. And, third, even with a suburban and city manager focus, income levels are, for a variety of reasons, much higher in the Bay Area. What we classify as a low-income community would more likely be a middle-income community in a national sample. Nevertheless, a good case can be made for calling our sample's bottom third low-income communities. In the Bay Area, these communities have in fact the lowest income and socioeconomic status. More important, all so-called low communities have less than 50 percent white-collar workers. And, almost without exception, these low-income communities are commonly identified as blue-collar or working-class cities.

Table 4–9
Relation of City Family Income Levels
to Policy Orientations

	Median Family Income of Cities		
Policy Orientation	$8,000 or higher High (N=18)	Between $6,800—$8,000 Medium (N=18)	$6,800 or less Low (N=18)
Political	39%	44%	69%
Administrative	61%	56%	31%

correlation seems to exist between high-income cities and Administrative orientations and low-income cities and Political orientations.

Consensus on What?

"Leadership for what?" we have not asked. City managers are all participants in the policy process. But beyond sheer activity, what do managers see as their civic mission. George Floro suggests that a dominant manager ethic is to do things that result in career mobility—moving to a more desirable city.[19] But what are the policy "things" a manager believes relevant or, put differently, what policy goals do managers articulate as important? City politics, despite the hopes of some, are not a matter of techniques and agreed services, but involve ends, values, and, for innovators, a vision of a better community.[20]

Policy goals unfortunately pose untidy analytical problems. City managers define policy goals in a particular political environment, where constraints of size, resources, or values influence if

[19]See George Floro, "Continuity in City-Manager Careers," *American Journal of Sociology*, 61 (November 1955), 240–46.

[20]In the classic text on organizations, *Functions of the Executive*, Chester Barnard says the essential executive functions are three: "first, to provide the system of communication; second, to promote the securing of essential efforts; and, third, to formulate and define purpose." Chester Barnard, *Functions of the Executive* (Cambridge, Mass.: Harvard University Press, 1938), p. 217. It is the third function that distinguishes city managers as policy makers. The question therefore becomes, toward what purposes does a city manager participate in the policy process?

not often dictate policy alternatives. Nevertheless, even a crude look at the policy goals of managers is important. In the field interviews, city managers were asked to discuss their most significant accomplishments—past or future: "As a city manager, what are the most important things you have or expect to accomplish?"

Deciding on common categories proved difficult. Some answers were largely irrelevant to any policy categories: "I can't say . . . I would have to discuss too many areas"; or "Staying here—most people thought I would not last six months." Others varied markedly in focus, level of abstraction, or in some cases on the manager's willingness to talk about himself. Yet, if manager responses are carefully analyzed, three general kinds of accomplishments stand out: administrative efficiency and effectiveness, those which center on improvements in procedures, services or staff; "bricks and mortar" results, those which refer to concrete capital expenditures; community destiny decisions, those which involve major planning, image, or growth decisions. While inexact in substance, these categories serve to highlight important manager policy goals.

The policy goals most closely associated with council-manager reform rhetoric are those of administrative efficiency and effectiveness. Almost three out of four managers (70%) mentioned at least one such accomplishment. The most typical responses are nearly verbatim quotes from National Municipal League handbooks:

> I would say a high level of administrative performance in city government . . . I mean efficiency, economy, and professionalization of various departments, viz., engineering, public works, fire, and police. . . . Economy covers a lot of things. I try to promote an economical government, to provide the highest amount of services for the lowest cost.

> I feel a serious obligation to keep city operations at an efficient level in providing services, to continue the level of services we now have, and to maintain home rule.

> Well, going into the past, the most important accomplishments have been financial policies which have resulted in improving the city plant.

Administrative improvements nevertheless include, among others, the building of a good staff—a noteworthy achievement. One of the Bay Area's most visible managers explained, "I think my most important accomplishment, although it is difficult to measure, is the building up of a highly qualified, well-paid staff. While there have been some squabbles over recommendations, there has never been any question either about the integrity or accuracy of the staff. While in many cities, the turnover is high and quality is low, in our city we have a superior staff." But, in general, administrative accomplishments center on procedural or fiscal activities that are of more direct consequence to the internal workings of city government than to the community or its citizenry.

Bricks and mortar accomplishments refer to discrete capital expenditures, for many managers (53%) express pride in public works projects. Managers' well-known penchant for concrete policy results is aptly illustrated by their interest in city building programs: "I think," stated one manager, "a city manager feels the most important thing is the development he makes in public works and how this relates to the general welfare. Public works applies to such as sewers, streets, water. How better can you serve all the people than through this department of government." More so than most policy decisions, the presence of firehouses or parks, for example, can be seen and accounted for by the personal choices of the manager. In most cities, capital improvements are routine, within the discretion of city government and more a product of growth than any vision of a better community. However, in some instances, capital improvements can have a major impact in a community. To take a famous example, Mayor Richard C. Lee's urban renewal in New Haven could not by any standard be called routine. The bricks and mortar results cited by a small-town city manager are likewise significant accomplishments:

> Let me preface what I will say with the comment that I have accomplished none of this by myself—other people are involved. One of the projects I was connected with was the one and a half million dollar bond issue passed two years ago. We will now have a new civic center and library. This will be one of the finest small town civic centers in the country. Another was a bond issue passed for a new fire station. A third project is the construction of the plaza on the SP property. I think my most important achievement is the acquisition of the SP property. The purchase is important for

many reasons: will develop new streets, build a plaza, build a Post
Office, provide off street parking, provide easements for store drive-
ways, and will sell parts to make purchase self-sustaining.

Beyond adding to city service facilities, these managers hope to
enhance or reshape the economic and social life of the community.

Community destiny decisions refer to major accomplishments
focused on the city-at-large as opposed to specific government
activities. With the fervor of elected executives, many managers
(63%) cited decisions that set directions and goals for the city:
promotion of master plans, cultivation of community identity,
recruitment of industry and/or commercial retailers, and the like.
These managers feel obligated to politick for the good life as well
as an efficient administration. Seeing the community as "my city,"
a significant number of managers attempt to define or at least
help define the goals, economic, social, and political, for *their*
community.

While managers articulate many of the same general achievements, one noteworthy difference emerged in the field interviews.
The emphases of the policy types are nearly dichotomous. Political managers focus on the impact of accomplishments for the
community:

> Don't think I could not specify buildings, yards, and streets. But
> my central concern and hopefully accomplishment is to integrate
> a disharmonious community, to soften it, to blend warring elements,
> and to build a community's self respect. I want to make the city
> hall in its corporate sense a respected institution. When I came
> here the paper was vitriolic. I was immediately accused of accepting
> a bribe. The hostility of the paper has lessened; I have turned it
> into an asset. I have tried to achieve a unity in which councilmen
> can agree. I have tried to establish a general morality for city em-
> ployees. I am concerned about the public response to our image. I
> have tried to make every community in which I have been city
> manager a balanced community. I see myself as a leader, a promoter.
> Rather than concentrate on management techniques, I see my job
> as being much broader in scope. We hope to develop a convention
> area, a commercial area, and an industrial area. We are now land
> rich. I am pushing a large development program. This is why I will
> remain here for the foreseeable future.
>
> First, I would say the most important accomplishment has been
> to keep up with and in many respects ahead of the city's growth.

This includes maintaining such services as libraries, parks, sewer treatment, storm drainage, fire houses, etc. . . . All this has been accomplished without increasing taxes—in fact, taxes have decreased. Second, we have been among the leaders in the approach to racial matters. We set up a Social Relations Commission—the first in the state. Third, we have set up long range community development programs, especially for capital investments. Fourth, we have been among the first in the nation to pioneer the sister city ideal. And fifth, we have built the city aggressively. From 17 square miles, we expect to become one of the largest cities in northern California, both in area and in population. This has not been easy.

No matter what the specific accomplishments, then, the emphases tend to be broad in scope, with city managers assuming the position of policy makers for the community.

In contrast, Administrative managers describe their accomplishments within the cast of the efficiency-effectiveness model found in the good books on civic reform:

I think the biggest accomplishment has been fiscal. I have restored a balanced budget to both cities in which I have been a city manager. This had not been done before. And I think this has been accomplished without hurting the level of services. This is the biggest thing. Second, we have built a number of parks and fire stations. The town has been asleep for 100 years. It is now beginning to grow again and we hope to be ready.

When I accepted the appointment here, we had a rather cloudy fame. Some questions arose as to the integrity of the city staff. In other words, the image of the city manager was tainted. This has been changed. I think this is my single most important contribution. As to accomplishments, we have a different yardstick for the community. We are not interested in increasing the sales tax or promoting industrial expansion. We hope to provide the necessary services at modest levels for minimal costs. Too, I try to protect our interests from forces without. We want to maintain our character and integrity.

These differences in personal policy objectives among Political and Administrative managers could importantly influence the character of policy decisions and thus the nature and fate of a community.

Chapter 5

Policy Role: Views of City Councilmen

The city council is the manager's decisive "significant other." Unlike other American legislators, city councilmen hire and fire the chief executive. These sanctions ensure that the pleasure of the council will largely determine a city manager's personal discretion and policy activities. Council acceptance—or at least acquiescence—becomes the base line for policy innovation and leadership by the city manager. Moreover, the council chamber serves as the legislative arena where councilmen, in effect, act as gatekeepers of policy changes in the community.

The importance of city councilmen for a manager's policy behavior is further enhanced because of the intimate exchanges between manager and councilmen. In council meetings, informal working sessions, private meetings, or individual conversations the city manager is subject to the continuous face-to-face influence of the council. The success or failure of a city manager notably depends on the personal rapport he develops and sustains with the members of his council. In addition, the city manager spends an estimated 30 to 40 percent of his time in meetings, carrying out instructions, and preparing reports for the council.[1]

This chapter will focus, therefore, on the policy views of city councilmen. What do they believe a city manager should do in

---

[1]For an excellent introduction to influence and interaction within small groups, see George Homans, *Social Behavior: Its Elementary Forms* (New York: Harcourt, Brace & World, 1961), especially pp. 112–45, 283–316.

terms of the policy process in a community? The assumption is, of course, that these views are as critical influences on policy behavior as the manager's own definition of his policy role.

The Official View

The official rhetoric on the division of labor on policy matters has not significantly changed from the original conception of the dichotomy between politics and administration. For example, the ICMA *Handbook for Councilmen* (prepared by "Veteran Councilmen as a Guide for New Councilmen and as a Reference Manual for Experienced Members of Local Legislative Bodies") explains: "The most important aspect of local government is policy making and this duty rests exclusively with the council when it operates under the council-manager plan. On the other hand, the chief duty of the city manager is the administration of policy."[2] Later, in more detail, the *Handbook* goes on to describe the proper relationship between councils and managers as follows:

> Of all the relationships existing throughout council-manager government, none is more important than that of the council and the manager. The basic and legal relationship generally is outlined either in state law or city charter. However, the success or failure of the plan in a large measure depends upon the working relationship that exists between the representative council and the professional manager.
>
> The manager is responsible to the council for proper conduct of all city activities under his direction. He provides the council with information and advice and makes recommendations. He is the council's technical advisor and consultant, but only the council can make laws and establish policies. Thus the burden for political leadership falls squarely on the council while the manager is primarily concerned with administrative leadership.[3]

These comments accurately represent the official viewpoint of such groups as ICMA and the National Municipal League. Orthodoxy

---

[2]*Handbook for Councilmen* (Chicago: International City Managers' Association, 1964), p. 1.
[3]*Ibid.*, p. 28.

instructs the individual councilman that he is responsible for city policy decisions.

Thus, city councilmen are prompted by the official ideology of the city manager plan to evaluate the city manager in terms of the classic reform principle of the dichotomy between politics and administration. Admittedly, the official statements of what a city manager should do also include such proper activities as providing information, preparing regular reports, drawing up the budget, identifying problems—present and future, formulating recommendations, and offering advice when asked. Nevertheless, though these activities are at the core of the policy process, the obvious role of the city manager as a policy participant is not explicitly stated in so many words.[4] (While most city managers are quick to debunk the politics-administration dichotomy in private, few city managers attempt to attack the dichotomy before members of their council.)

Views of City Councilmen

To examine how city councilmen interpret the proper policy activities of the city manager, the primary emphasis will be on interview results. Bay Area councilmen were asked: "Now, what about the city manager? What should he do, or not do, to be most effective in his relations with the Council? How about on policy matters?" Responses to this question were coded—up to five per councilman—into appropriate policy activities for the city manager. The content and direction of councilmen policy views will thus be identified by answers to the above open-ended question (Table 5-1).

City Manager as Staff Adviser

Councilmen espouse the policy style hallowed by official rhetoric, namely, the staff administrator. Time after time, city council-

---

[4]For a general description of the "most essential and characteristic functions" of a chief executive, see Edward Banfield, "The Training of the Executive," in *Public Policy,* Carl Friedrich and Seymour Harris, eds. (Cambridge, Mass.: Harvard University Press, 1960), pp. 27–28.

Table 5–1

Councilmen Views of Proper Policy Activities
for the City Manager

Proper Policy Activities	Percentage of Councilmen Who Mention Each Activity (N = 371)
1. Be a good administrator	52
2. Leave policy to council	47
3. Give good advice	46
4. Keep council informed	39
5. Work with council as a team	30
6. Identify policy problems	27
7. Be a good diplomat for city	24
8. Be a professional	20
9. Avoid intracouncil politics	14
10. Be a good public relations man for council	13

men define the proper policy activities of the city manager in terms of his formal duties and powers. No other major interpretation of city councilmen responses is possible; for they express strong preference for a staff officer hired to give advice and to implement council policy.

To be specific, let us take up the four activities most frequently mentioned. The city manager should first be a good administrator; that is, he should maintain a smooth-running administration and effectively carry out council policy. Because the city manager is the resident administrator, this citation of his most conspicuous formal obligation should probably be expected. However noteworthy, the emphasis on what makes a good administrator is not the abstract criteria of reform government but rather implementing the specific policies and general philosophy of the city council:

> The city manager is the person delegated to implement the actions taken by the council and the general feelings of the council with respect to management.

> The city manager should recognize his position as one of both accepting responsibility and passing to the council for directions in decisions. The council is the policy making body. He is merely to carry out their policies.

Second, in one way or another, many councilmen were quick to point out that a city manager should avoid direct involvement in the policy and political process of the city. This conviction is often emphatically stated:

> He should not try to set policy. PERIOD! He should not try to act as a sixth councilman. To the contrary—just carry out the policy as set by the council.

> He should stay out of politics and be a good administrator. The making of policy should rest without question with the council and the manager should carry them out.

Other councilmen, if less dogmatically, would find cause to stress the subordinate role of the manager. The manager is warned, exhorted, and even commanded to leave major policy and political questions to the council. He is not seen as a political executive but rather as one "who should be very cautious to obtain the consent of the majority of the councilmen before changing or deciding anything of any magnitude." Among city councilmen, claims for policy advocacy and leadership by city managers find few adherents and many foes.

Finally, the third and fourth responses suggest that city councilmen expect a city manager to give advice and information. For most city councilmen recognize that information and advice are required in order to make policy decisions. Councilmen have important positive as well as negative rules for the city manager. They indicate, for example, that the manager should be prepared to answer all questions, to give first-rate policy advice, and to keep the council well informed on all problems facing the city. Further, the adviser skills of the city manager become a major factor in how he is evaluated by city councilmen; in the words of one councilman, "Informing . . . keeping us informed of his activities as well as problems that are generated. This is the most important thing a city manager can do—and in our case, we have an effective city manager because he does just that."

City Manager as Political Tribune

Many city councilmen nevertheless recognize the reputation of city hall and even the city council depends on the political skills of the city manager. Some councilmen note that the city manager should alert them to possible troubles or to new programs and/or when necessary take an active part in policy decisions. More generally, city councilmen expect the city manager to be a composite spokesman, salesman, and representative for the council. The city manager should, as expressed by one councilman, "do whatever is necessary to make the council look good." The point to make is that the city manager is expected to be the policy champion and public representative of the city council (Table 5–1, especially items 5 to 10).

Yet these views of the city manager as a political tribune do not fundamentally clash with the primary definition of the city manager as a staff adviser. The council mandate is for harmony, cooperation, and, if at all possible, avoiding contentious issues. Some of the strongest statements in the interviews with councilmen are those objecting to personal policy leadership by the manager. While the manager can initiate, even recommend various policies, he faces clear restrictions on how he can politick for their approval. As one councilman explained, "The city manager must conduct himself as a professional man. . . . The best thing is to be prepared for each meeting. He'd better watch himself and not meddle, that's the most dangerous thing he can do." Thus, though the list of expectations for the city manager found in Table 5–1 suggests possible differences of opinion on what a city manager should do on policy matters, the results, in fact, clarify rather than challenge the central conception of the city manager as a staff adviser to the council. The city manager should, in short, represent the council and not present or lobby for an executive policy program.

What Kind of Participant?

Variations do exist, however, in how city councilmen define the city manager's policy role. Councilmen range from those who object to all policy activity to a few who exhort the manager to be a complete policy executive. For example, one articulate but exceptional councilman expressed the following view:

> The city manager should use the best judgment at his command. There are those who say the manager does not make policy. I don't

agree with that position. Every decision he makes, every recommendation he makes to the council is, in a way, policy making. So it would seem to me that he should be intellectually honest and have the good of the city uppermost in his mind. I also feel that he should not be overly concerned about what he thinks is the council's point of view as a basis for policy discussions. I am afraid I don't have much stock in the notion that the manager is a kind of mechanical administrator—he has, and should, share in policy making.

To examine the range and distribution of various policy views, all councilmen were classified into five categories based on the extent to which each favored policy participation on the part of the manager (Table 5–2). The levels at which councilmen will approve policy participation confirm the noted emphasis that the city manager should participate as a staff adviser—carry out policies, supply information, anticipate and research problems, and occasionally propose policies or solutions. Those councilmen who endorse an activist role for the manager are few in number. And even those councilmen do not view the city manager as a political executive with policy privileges independent of the council—as one such councilman observed, "The council should keep hands off the manager while he tends to his duties, but he must keep the council informed of important matters that occur. He must adhere to policy guide lines which are established. . . . He must be knowledgeable and responsive to the directions of the council." However, the image of the staff adviser does reflect somewhat differing emphases and interpretations, and these differences should not be ignored for they could influence what a city manager may do in formulating or recommending policy. For levels of policy participation endorsed by councilmen limit the city manager and prescribe what he can do in the city policy process.

Policy Views: The Consensus

Whether a consensus exists among city councilmen on a limited policy role definition for city managers can perhaps most accurately be measured by closed responses. For that purpose, we asked ten questions more or less comparable to those asked of city managers: "Here are some statements which reflect different

Table 5–2
Levels of Approved Policy Participation

A City Manager Should:	Percentage of Councilmen Who Approve (N = 363)
1. Carry out policy	100
2. Supply information	89
3. Anticipate and research problems	73
4. Propose policies or solutions	48
5. Be a policy leader	14

viewpoints about the job of city manager or top administrator. We would like to know how you feel about these viewpoints. Would you please read each one and then check just how much you generally agree or disagree with it" (Table 5–3).

The general agreement demonstrated on seven of the ten items further confirms that the predominant interpretation of councilmen is that of a narrow definition of the city manager's policy role. Noteworthy, the councilmen indicate the highest level of agreement on the classic dichotomy between politics and administration—almost nine out of ten councilmen ratify the reform rhetoric that "the city manager should act as administrator and leave policy matters to the council." Thus, when directly asked, city councilmen overwhelmingly reject overt policy participation by the city manager.

More generally, councilmen consistently limit the proper policy activities of the city manager to those of staff administrator and council adviser. Claims to policy or community leadership are rejected. Councilmen insist that city managers not work through the power structure but rather informally with the council. Agreement is readily achieved on prohibitions against participation in council elections. Councilmen do accept policy advocacy *if necessary* but prefer—by small margins—that a city manager remain neutral on divisive issues, avoid controversial policy proposals, and abstain from political leadership. As a final example, the executive budget is one prerogative city managers have increasingly assumed—many cities have such a statute on the books. How-

Table 5–3
City Councilmen Policy Views of the City Manager

| | Percentages | |
Questions	Agree	Disagree
1. *Policy Administrator*—The city manager should act as an administrator and leave policy matters to the council. (N = 350)	87	13
2. *Political Leader*—The city manager should work through the most powerful members of the community to achieve his policy goals. (N = 353)	15	85
3. *Political Campaigner*—The city manager should give a helping hand to good councilmen who are coming up for re-election. (N = 350)	17	83
4. *Necessary Policy Advocate*—The city manager should advocate major changes in city policies if necessary. (N = 348)	82	18
5. *Informal Policy Advocate*—The city manager should work informally with councilmen to prepare important policy proposals. (N = 348)	80	20
6. *Political Recruiter*—The city manager should encourage people whom he respects to run for the council. (N = 348)	22	78
7. *Policy Neutral*—The city manager should maintain a neutral stand on any issues which may divide the community. (N = 349)	63	37
8. *Policy Leader*—The city manager should assume leadership in shaping municipal affairs. (N = 347)	43	57
9. *Policy Advocate*—The city manager should advocate policies even if important parts of the community seem hostile to them. (N = 344)	47	53
10. *Budget Consultant*—The city manager should consult with the council before drafting his own budget proposal. (N = 350)	49	51

ever, even on this activity only a hairline majority of councilmen
favor such an arrangement.

Variations in Policy Views

Although councilmen generally agree among themselves on the
proper relation of the city manager to the policy process, there
are sufficient differences among them to permit more detailed
analysis. These differences are important; for they suggest that
managers in different cities face different councilmanic expectations. Moreover, the different role definitions among managers
themselves might be shaped by the degree of freedom permitted
them by the councilmen with whom they work.

Patterned differences in councilmen views of the city manager
can be found in their responses to the ten questions in Table 5–3.
Each city councilman was indexed and classified according to the
rules developed for typing the policy orientations of city managers (see Chapter three).[5] When the response scores of city
councilmen were compared with the policy orientations of city
managers, the results seemed at first to show only the major
differences between councilmen and managers. More than eight
out of ten city councilmen agree upon an Administrative orientation (Director or Technician). Yet, a more careful study of the
distribution of city councilmen scores indicated that a large number do not endorse even the most limited definition expressed by

---

[5]In substance, each councilman's responses are added together and the conse-
quent score becomes a measure of his conception of the manager's policy role.
Clearly the rules and closed questions are biased in favor of a broad definition
of the policy role by city councilmen. For one, city managers had to choose
from: strongly agree, tend to agree, tend to disagree, and strongly disagree.
Councilmen could select from: agree, tend to agree, tend to disagree, and disagree. These options are such that "agree" is a much easier choice than
"strongly agree" and so forth. And, second, two of the councilmen questions
(item 4 Necessary Policy Advocate and item 5 Informal Policy Advocate) are
worded in a manner as to evoke a positive response to a manager's involvement in the policy process. Nevertheless, despite these differences, councilmen and manager scores on similar closed questions present a useful format for
identifying, comparing, and interpreting major variations in the policy views of
city councilmen.

city managers. To take this perspective into account, a third
Administrative orientation was introduced, that of Assistant.[6]
Councilmen views thus vary, but primarily within a range established by a limited view of the policy role of the city manager:

Policy Orientations for Manager		Number of Councilmen
Political		64
	Political Leader 11	
	Political Executive 53	
	64	
Administrative		287
	Administrative Director 81	
	Administrative Technician 101	
	Administrative Assistant 105	
	287	

Nevertheless, the variations in councilmen's views represent
major, and, to some extent, quite different perspectives on the
proper policy activities of the city manager. These expectation
differences among councilmen are well illustrated by average
responses to the ten closed questions (Table 5–4). No view is expressed with more clarity than that of Assistant. The motif that
"the city manager should follow policy set by the council" domi-
nates every response. Even the question, "The city manager
should advocate major changes in city policies if necessary," pro-
vokes marked disagreement. Strong objections are recorded on
any question favoring policy discretion on the part of the manager; as one councilman explained, "The city manager is the man
who administers the policies set forth by the council. If he doesn't,
he won't stay around. And we insist that our policies be carried
out."

Councilmen who contend that managers should be Technicians also resolutely defend the politics-administration dichot-

---

[6]See Appendix C-2.

Table 5–4
Average Responses of City Councilmen
with Differing Policy Views to the Ten Closed Questions

| | AVERAGE RESPONSES OF CITY COUNCILMEN* | | | |
| | Political Leader/ | Administrative | | |
Questions	Executive $\overline{\text{X}}$	Director $\overline{\text{X}}$	Technician $\overline{\text{X}}$	Assistant $\overline{\text{X}}$
1. Policy Administrator	+0.8	+1.9	+2.2	+2.8
2. Political Leader	−0.5	−1.1	−1.9	−2.7
3. Political Campaigner	−0.9	−1.5	−1.8	−2.7
4. Necessary Policy Advocate	+2.5	+2.1	+1.8	−0.1
5. Informal Policy Advocate	+2.1	+2.1	+0.8	+0.6
6. Political Recruiter	0.0	−1.1	−1.5	−2.5
7. Policy Neutral	−1.0	0.0	+0.9	+2.0
8. Policy Leader	+1.5	+0.2	−0.6	−2.4
9. Policy Advocate	+1.4	+0.8	+0.2	−1.9
10. Budget Consultant	−0.3	−0.2	+0.1	0.0

*Councilmen responses were translated into numerical scores as follows: agree +3; tend to agree +1; tend to disagree −1; and disagree −3.

omy. One major difference, however, with their colleagues who choose the Assistant role is a stated willingness to let the city manager run city hall: "He should stay out of policy. We draw the line. At the same time, he draws it for us so we stay out of administration." Also, they show some hint of a more flexible definition of the manager's policy role. Managers, for example, are occasionally encouraged to propose policy changes. Nevertheless, these councilmen overwhelmingly agree that the city manager "should remember that he is working for the council. And his only reason to exist is to serve us."

Councilmen who assert that a manager should be a Director likewise lay claim to a narrow definition of the manager's policy role. These councilmen insist that the manager act as an administrator and not as a policy maker. Yet, while wary of political activity, they endorse the role of the manager as a policy adviser. The manager is seen as a source for information and, occasionally, recommendations; for example, in the words of one such councilman, "The city manager should present all the facts that he can muster and as soon and concisely as possible. He should level with the council. He shouldn't be a policy maker. Instead, just truthful in advising us." Though ambivalent on what discretion a policy adviser should have, these councilmen approve—if narrowly—the participation of the manager in the policy process: he should advocate policy, if necessary, or be an informal policy advocate, and so forth. It should be observed, however, that participation is defined in terms of service to the council rather than problem solving.

Finally, less than one out of five councilmen believe that a manager should be an Executive or a Leader. These councilmen recognize and endorse the involvement of the city manager in the policy process. Though they agree that "the city manager should act as an administrator," these councilmen indicate on almost every other closed question that they prefer a strong city manager. They believe a city manager should be both advocate and leader; and almost half even hold that a city manager can, perhaps should, recruit councilmen he would like on the city council. The unanimous conviction is that the city manager should not leave policy matters to the council, or, as one councilman stated:

> He should not be afraid to make recommendations, and give reasons for, on matters voted on by the council. He should not become involved, but can be concerned, with political power plays on the council. And he must know the city. He must be able to negotiate with industry, the county, and the state.

Sources of Variations

Though my research interests are not in explaining why councilmen differ in their views of the appropriate role of managers, it is useful to determine whether marked patterns occur from one type of city to the next.[7] Table 5–5 shows that the differing views

---

[7] No analysis of why city councilmen hold differing policy views will be attempted. From conversations with other members of the City Council Project, personal factors would appear quite complex and often tied to historical and situational characteristics of the community. See Kenneth Prewitt, *The Recruitment of Political Leaders: A Study of Citizen Politicians* (Indianapolis: Bobbs-Merrill, 1970).

Table 5-5
Relation of Three Community Characteristics to Councilmen Policy Views of the City Manager

Policy Views	Community Size			Community Income		
	Small (0–10,000)	Medium (10–50,000)	Large (50,000+)	Low ($6,749–)	Middle ($6,750–7,750)	High ($7,751+)
Assistant	33	28	29	28	22	36
Technician	25	30	29	29	32	26
Director	23	26	24	22	29	20
Politico	19	16	18	21	17	18
	100% (126)	100% (135)	100% (87)	100% (97)	100% (100)	100% (122)

	Community Function		
	Employing	Balanced	Dormitory
Assistant	38	24	30
Technician	26	29	30
Director	18	28	22
Politico	18	19	18
	100% (71)	100% (92)	100% (186)

of the city manager held by councilmen are randomly distributed across different types of cities, at least insofar as size, wealth, and function identify different types of city.[8] The only pattern is a very slight tendency for small upper-class communities to have councilmen who stress the Assistant conception of the city manager role. For the most part, councilmen's views of the appropriate role of the city manager show no clear ties to any kind of city: large or small, rich or poor, employing or dormitory. Rather, in the cities studied, most councilmen have adopted prescriptions to limit policy ventures on the part of the manager. In fact, only in one city did a majority of councilmen hold Political views for the manager's role—and this city has a population of less than twenty-five hundred people. Thus, the analysis indicates that city councils in almost all Bay Area communities are probably vigorous champions of their own policy supremacy.

---

[8]Speculation has outdistanced research in accounting for differing policy views among city councilmen. Numerous community characteristics have been cited that could make a difference. Probably no characteristics have been more frequently discussed than those of size, income, and function of a city. Size is a shorthand measure of socioeconomic and political complexity. Income measures identify the supposed consumer preferences of city residents. Robert Wood found that if you knew the median income and density you have a better predictor of the public policies of a city than any of the more customary political factors. See Robert Wood, *1400 Governments* (Cambridge, Mass.: Harvard University Press, 1961). And function is one of the most widely used classification schemes in the search for order in metropolitan variety. See, for example, the discussion of Duncan and Reiss on the importance of functional activity for explaining differences among communities: Otis Duncan and Albert Reiss, *Social Characteristics of Urban and Rural Communities, 1950* (New York: John Wiley & Sons, 1956), especially pp. 5–18, 215–52. These three variables were thus selected to see if major community characteristics may account for differing manager views expressed by city councilmen.

Chapter 6

Consensus and Conflict Between Manager and Council

City managers and city councilmen hold notably different conceptions of the policy role of the city manager. The lack of interposition consensus should perhaps be anticipated. For one, the city manager occupies an interstitial position that is open to challenge and interpretation. (An interstitial position is one for which "significant others" are located in different social systems from the focal person.) The city manager spends much of his time in interaction with people other than the city council. How he engages and persuades the administrative staff, business-men, good government people, special interest groups, public-at-large, as well as the city council, will largely determine his success as a city manager. These groups present the manager with self-interest demands and, as a result, hold differing expectations of what a city manager should do on policy matters. Thus, be-cause the city manager offers a major focus for group conflicts, it is likely that the city manager's policy role would be subject to acute and chronic disagreement.

Moreover, the city manager plays a major innovative role in the city; for regardless of his own views, circumstances require him to become a proponent of change. The city manager is obliged to involve himself in the constant improvement of city services and the identification of city problems and their solutions.[1] And, in proposing policy changes, the city manager will invariably find groups in opposition, including at times his own council. These policy clashes can be translated as new guard (innovation) versus old guard (status quo). The importance of these conflicts should not be minimized, for as explained by Robert Kahn and colleagues in *Organizational Stress:*

> In organizations the "accepted" policy is accepted by definition and bolstered by precedent and ideology. The newly created policy must be justified prior to its acceptance. Organizations vary considerably in their receptivity to change, but it is the change and not the status quo which must be newly justified.[2]

The innovative activities of the city manager become, in other words, a major source of conflicting role interpretations because these activities frequently challenge the accepted views of the council or other community groups.

On the other hand, while most occupants of interstitial and innovation positions face major role conflicts, the city manager is distinguished by his close relations, formal and informal, with city councilmen. Council members can directly inspect and review the manager's activities. In no obvious way can he establish much distance between himself and councilmen; and at the minimum, he must have their informed approval of any major policy action. Perhaps more important, the city manager is hired to take orders and follow the values of the council: failure to satisfy council expectations can provoke sanctions that are real, immediate, and decisive. Role pressures from councilmen are, in substance, near requisite to policy decisions, and backed by strong sanctions.

This chapter will therefore examine the conflicting views of managers and councilmen on the policy role of the city manager in order to analyze and evaluate four questions: What is the character and extent of the policy role conflict? Why does the conflict exist? Is the conflict myth or fact? And what are the policy consequences of the conflict's resolution?

---

[1]For an extended discussion of the city manager as a proponent of change, see Chapter two, especially pp. 23–31.

[2]Robert Kahn, Donald Wolfe, Robert Quinn, and J. Diedrick Snoek, *Organizational Stress: Studies in Role Conflict and Ambiguity* (New York: John Wiley & Sons, 1964), p. 125.

Policy Role Conflict

Striking disagreements exist between managers and councilmen on what the city manager should do on policy matters. City managers largely hold the policy values of the political executive—they are interested in formulating and defining the purpose of city government.[3] City councilmen, for the most part, regard the city manager as their man in city hall who administers the city and who is on tap for advice, information, and recommendations. The extent of this conflict in role interpretation is perhaps best demonstrated by the responses of managers and councilmen to identical questions on the limits and directions of the manager's policy role (Table 6–1).

The differences in responses on selected policy activities illustrate the kind and extent of potential conflict between managers and councilmen. Many of these disagreements center on the fundamental character of the city manager's participation in the policy process and, as such, cannot be dismissed as unimportant role differences. Rather, the results suggest that managers and councilmen often subscribe to two nearly mutually exclusive conceptions of the policy role.

The extent of role conflict between managers and councilmen, however, may be an artifact of the analysis. Because responses of managers and councilmen have each been aggregated, evidence of policy role conflict between a specific manager and his council has not been examined. Perhaps the policy conceptions of city managers are to some extent related to the views of their own councilmen. Managers, for example, who hold a broad view of the policy role could serve in cities that have councils who also endorse a relatively active policy role for the manager. If true, the role conflict between managers and councilmen has been exaggerated, and thus the significance of the role clash would be much less serious.

No such interpretation, however, is warranted, for no matter how the data are analyzed, the policy views of the manager and his

---

[3]See Philip Selznick, *Leadership in Administration* (New York: Harper & Row, 1957), especially pp. 29–64.

Table 6–1
Manager and Councilmen: Conflicts in Policy Role Views

Items	City Managers Percentage Agree	(*Difference*)	City Councilmen Percentage Agree
1. *Policy Administrator*—"A city manager should act as an administrator and leave policy matters to the council."	22	(66)	88
2. *Policy Innovator*—"A city manager should assume leadership in shaping municipal policies."	88	(46)	42
3. *Political Leader*—"A city manager should work through the most powerful members of the community to achieve policy goals."	53	(41)	12
4. *Policy Neutral*—"A city manager should maintain a neutral stand on any issues on which the community is divided."	24	(40)	64
5. *Political Recruiter*—"A city manager should encourage people whom he respects to run for city council."	44	(21)	23
6. *Budget Consultant*—"A city manager should consult with the council before drafting his own budget."	31	(18)	49

council do not decisively converge. Two measures can illustrate. First, the policy views of the city councilmen are examined in terms of the policy orientations of their own city managers. This measure should indicate the extent to which role definitions of councilmen and managers are related—for example, are councilmen in cities with Political managers more likely to hold Political views (Table 6–2)? When compared, no pronounced patterns are disclosed; instead, it would seem to make little difference what

Table 6–2
Views of City Councilmen and the Orientations
of Their Managers

| Orientations of Their Managers | *Views of City Councilmen* | | | | | |
	Assistant	Technician	Director	Politico	Percent	Number
Administrative Technician	18*	35	20	27	100	44
Administrative Director	35	27	19	19	100	63
Political Executive	32	22	32	14	100	72
Political Leader	29	31	20	20	100	56

*Table reads, for example, 18 percent of city councilmen with Administrative Technicians as managers hold Assistant views.

kind of policy views managers or councilmen have for one another. For the results suggest that the views of managers and
councilmen are not interdependent influences on each other's
policy role conceptions.

Second, and perhaps a better measure, the policy views of city
councils—rather than city councilmen—can be examined in terms
of their manager's policy orientations. To establish a council's
policy view, an average of the policy views of three or more members of the same council were calculated.[4] Again, the results show
that there is little tendency for policy views to converge. To the
contrary, most managers face councils that object to their conception of the policy role. In substance, therefore, the evidence
indicates that managers and councilmen are likely to hold sharply
conflicting views of the manager's policy role (Table 6–3).

---

[4]To examine views of the manager's policy role held by city councils rather than
by city councilmen, councilmen scores on the ten closed questions were again
used (see Chapter five, pp. 84–87). This time, however, for every council with
at least a majority of its councilmen interviewed, the total response scores of
their councilmen were added up and then averaged. Employing the same criteria used to type councilmen, the city councils were classified accordingly as
having Assistant, Technician, Director, or Politico views of the manager's policy
role.

Table 6–3
Views of City Councils and the Orientations
of Their Managers

Orientations of Their Managers	*Views of City Councils*					
	Assistant	Technician	Director	Politico	Percent	Number
Administrative Technician	0	67	22	11	100	9
Administrative Director	28	36	36	0	100	14
Political Executive	12	69	19	0	100	16
Political Leader	17	42	33	8	100	12

An Explanation for Conflict

The major policy role conflicts that exist between managers and councilmen are rooted in personal and positional differences. Three such differences call for discussion. First, recruitment and socialization patterns are markedly dissimilar. City managers are self-recruited in college for a career in public service, many receive academic training in public administration, and almost all spend some years as an apprentice in city management.[5] These

---

[5]The ideal background for entry into a career in city management can be found in the admissions criteria for the Fels Institute of Local and State Government at the University of Pennsylvania: "Briefly put, this is the type of student we desire:

1) He should have a sufficiently mature disposition and habit of life so that taxpayers will not hesitate to repose confidence in him and assign him responsible duties.

2) He should be eager to advance rapidly as a public administrator but not in political or party life. Nor should he have as his primary objective large pecuniary rewards.

3) He should be able to command the respect of his employers and associates for his academic ability and professional attainments, but it is more important that he be able to win the support of initially unsympathetic people through his modesty, self-effacement, and sincerity.

4) He should be in the upper fifth of his classes, scholastically.

5) He should feel that one of the most pressing social and political problems

experiences foster commitments to the public interest and to a self-image as a policy maker. Most managers hope to make a difference in the community—and a difference usually requires active intervention in city government. For example, one manager expressed the wish of many when he indicated that if he had his way, he would bulldoze the entire city into San Francisco Bay and begin again. And this time, he emphasized, he would remedy the aesthetic, transportation, and functional problems he could not now resolve.[6] By contrast, councilmen follow no common institutional patterns of socialization or recruitment. Instead, the councilmen are elected and must perform within the traditional customs, interests, and ideology of a specific community.[7] The policy values that result often call for a commitment to the status quo, with few councilmen taking strong exception to the situation in which they find themselves. In almost every community, there is, in brief, a new guard (most city managers and some councilmen) advocating change and the old guard (most city councilmen and some city managers) supporting the status quo.[8] The role conflict can thus center on two per-

---

in the United States today is the improvement of government and administration at the local and state levels.

  6) He should have evinced a determination to enter upon a career of administrative leadership in local or state government."

[6]Frustrations are not unique to this manager. "The decisive feature of the practitioner's position," writes Leonard Reissman, "is almost complete lack of power to affect urban trends in any significant way. Confronted most of the time by the consequences of previously unplanned actions, he is further restricted to a narrow range of possible steps he can take to solve the problems they have raised. It is not that he lacks judgment or knowledge; he lacks the means to do almost anything of positive and lasting consequence. . . . The practitioner, who understands the total situation, must endure endless frustration." See Leonard Reissman, *The Urban Process* (New York: The Free Press, 1964), pp. 28–29, 38.

[7]City councilmen do, however, often share common background characteristics: see, for example, Eugene Lee, *Politics of Nonpartisanship* (Berkeley and Los Angeles: University of California Press, 1960), pp. 50–59; or Kenneth Prewitt, *The Recruitment of Political Leaders* (Indianapolis: Bobbs-Merrill, 1970).

[8]The innovative manager and status quo councilman dichotomy should not be overdrawn or strictly interpreted—as individuals, city managers are not saviors of cities and councilmen superannuated barriers to such salvation. There is, for example, great variation among Bay Area councilmen with respect to their policy attitudes and behavior. It is nonetheless likely that in most cities the city manager will be more liberal, cosmopolitan, and visionary than his councilmen.

spectives of the proper activities of city hall that are logical outcomes from different kinds of recruitment and socialization
experiences.

Second, though closely related to the first, differences in frames
of reference also merit citation. City managers are professionals.
They are bound by common norms and a code of ethics to make
decisions in the public interest. Few managers feel their primary
responsibility is to represent and promote the interests of councilmen. Rather, most managers share a cosmopolitan outlook focused primarily on a set of professional standards. These values
are accentuated by detailed information, staff pressures, awareness
of problems—local and national—and short tenure. The councilmen, by contrast, are amateurs. Their policy interests are typically
local in orientation and particularistic in emphasis. The manager
is conceived as a well-paid employee, expected to give unrequited
loyalty to the city, to be governed by the directives of the council,
and to accept the policy hopes and goals of councilmen—"city man-

However, beyond such personal attitudes, the policy functions of the city manager and his city councilmen call forth innovative and status quo perspectives on
sociopolitical change. For, as Clarence Ridley explains, "the character of council action has changed as the city manager and others in the administrative
organization make more of the recommendations for council consideration. The
council naturally depends on the manager and his staff to study the problems
and recommend solutions." Clarence Ridley, *The Role of the City Manager in
Policy Formulation* (Chicago: International City Managers' Association, 1958),
p. 52. The result, in short, is that the city manager and his staff—because of
their near-monopoly of technical competence—propose most policies and, in
turn, the city council disposes of them. Or, in other words, the city manager acts
as the policy advocate, while his councilmen serve as policy judges for the community. (Only fifteen out of forty Bay Area managers, when interviewed, took
exception to the statement, "The role of the council has emerged as a reviewing
and vetoing agency, checking upon the city manager more than leading him in
terms of policy making.") In practice, this advocate-judge relationship imposes
innovative responsibilities on the city manager and status quo responsibilities
on his city councilmen. Further, available evidence suggests that most city councils exhibit little innovation or leadership on policy matters and that their
major power appears to reside in the fact that their approval is needed. See
Duane Lockard, *Politics of State and Local Government* (2nd ed.; New York:
The Macmillan Company, 1969), pp. 297–98, for an excellent overview of the
powers and performance of city councils. Nevertheless, it should be recognized
that city councils can vary importantly in their receptivity to change, with
some city councils more willing to approve innovative policies than others, and
these differences can influence the kinds of public policies adopted by cities.

agers should be on tap and not on top." To recapitulate, the policy role conflicts between managers and councilmen can be partly explained by important differences in recruitment, socialization, and the frames of reference that result.[9]

The most important differences that account for the clashing role interpretations can be found in the tasks for which managers and councilmen are held accountable. In effect, managers are expected to recognize and take up the problems of the city. No matter what the rulebook says, the city managers have most of the responsibilities of an elected chief executive. Success or failure depends on the city's approach to problems, and inexorably this requires the manager to provide policy innovation and leadership. No one in the city has more public time, information, access, or visibility, and these factors thrust the manager forward to stand on his policy record. Circumstances literally require a manager to take an active as opposed to a passive view of the policy role.

City councilmen, on the other hand, are formally awarded the symbols and prerogatives of policy making. Sanctioned by law, rhetoric, and procedures, councilmen are the people's legal representatives and the city's legitimate makers of public decisions. They often campaign and are usually attacked on policy and not administrative matters. For example, a newspaper began a "throw the rascals out" editorial with these admonitions:

> It is doubtful that there is anywhere to go but up. For the present council has shown not a grain of leadership. Where civic progress has been made, it has come only as the result of, and reaction to, substantial citizen pressure. This is true whether one is considering the proposed master plan, the Downtown Mall, the Community Relations Commission, the youth center, or what have you. . . . Now it is time for the voters to reject these incumbent councilmen, and where it is at all possible, to turn them out of office.

The policy decisions of the city are the ultimate responsibility of the council, for which members have to answer to special interests

---

[9]For a clear and useful explication of the development of a perspective —such as the policy role—see Howard S. Becker, Blanche Geer, Everett Hughes, and Anselm Strauss, *Boys in White: Student Culture in Medical School* (Chicago: University of Chicago Press, 1961), pp. 33–48.

as well as the general public.[10] Thus, councilmen see the city manager in terms of services he can or should render for the council. In essence, therefore, the tasks for which managers (resolving problems) and councilmen (making policy) are held accountable make policy role conflicts unavoidable.

Policy Conflict and Its Resolution

Whatever the explanations for the contrasting definitions, many local government writers tend to dismiss such manager-council role differences as "image versus reality" conflicts. That is, while councilmen justify and explain the council-manager prerogatives in terms of the image of the manager as dealing primarily with administrative matters and leaving policy matters to the council, city managers—in practice—participate in most stages of the community political process.[11] Furthermore, most political scientists see the city manager as acquiring actual leadership and dominance in the determination of public policy. From this conclusion, the city manager is continually exhorted to "as-

---

[10]In a speech before the 1968 Mayors' and Councilmen's Institute, Jack Maltester, Mayor of San Leandro, carefully emphasized what most elected officials assume to be the fundamental policy responsibilities of city councilmen: "Remember, you face the voters for approval or disapproval of the city's policies, not the administrator. . . . From an operational standpoint, the line between policy and administration is not always clearly defined. Admittedly, there is a multi-shaded gray area requiring mutual cooperation, understanding, and respect. The danger lies in the chance that you . . . might delegate to the administrator some of the disagreeable political duties because of his full-time status and administrative knowledge. This *can only result* in a general reduction of status of the elected officers while placing the administrator in a position for which he is neither qualified nor constituted. Of course, in some instances, there are administrators who have a tendency to make policy and expect you to automatically approve of their decisions. This is certainly not a healthy situation and it can be corrected only by *you* assuming your obligations. So make your own policy decisions; you alone will have to answer to them, and a good administrator will see that they are carried out." Jack Maltester, "The City Council and Political Leadership," in *Proceedings Mayors' and Councilmen's Institute, Anaheim, May 19–22, 1968* (League of California Cities, 1968), pp. A-3, A-4.

[11]See, for example, Jeptha Carrell, *Role of the City Manager* (Kansas City, Mo.: Community Studies, 1962), pp. 15–16.

sume new responsibilities for leadership." John Pfiffner, for example, writes, "From now on the city manager will have to become more of a human or social engineer and less of an efficiency engineer in the traditional sense."[12] The underlying assumption, of course, is that the policy behavior of the manager is largely shaped by what he thinks the office should be.

Such explanations are, however, open to serious question, for they ignore or discount the policy expectations of the council for the city manager. Social scientists find political man enmeshed in a network of interpersonal exchanges. Political behavior is better understood as a process in which the person shapes and controls his conduct by taking into account the expectations of others with whom he interacts. And evidence further suggests that most people, including councilmen, behave in terms of the meaning they give their politics. The principal argument here is that conflicting interpretations of the policy role—specifically between managers and councilmen—are central to explanations of the policy behavior of city managers.

Fact, Not Fiction

The policy relations between the manager and his councilmen are not limited to a set of formal exchanges but occasion instead a full spectrum of interpersonal and political problems. In even routine circumstances, status and expertise differences would play havoc in sustaining a satisfactory working relationship. Yet on important policy matters the possibilities for conflict are further enhanced. Jeptha Carrell identifies six kinds of conflict between managers and councilmen: power prerogatives, personality clashes, political setting, policy expediency differences, manager's inflexibility and rectitude, and communication and cognition difficulties.[13] Close analysis of these six sources of friction reveals that with perhaps one exception, actual conflict centers on how

---

[12]John Pfiffner, "The Job of the City Manager," *Public Management,* 43 (June 1961), 123.
[13]Jeptha Carrell, "The City Manager and His Council: Sources of Conflict," *Public Administration Review,* 21 (December 1962), 203–8.

managers and councilmen each define and accept the policy definitions of the other. Several studies indicate the same: role conflicts over what a city manager should do or say represent most of the important sources of policy tensions between managers and their councilmen.

Beyond assertion, varied evidence exists for the importance of the policy role conflict. First, role analysis would indicate that the city council exerts powerful pressures on the manager—members can invoke legitimate and coercive powers as well as provide inducements to secure role compliance. To investigate relative concern for the city council, city managers were asked to rank six groups—administrative staff, fellow city managers, public-at-large, community groups, professional management groups, and council—according to their importance to the manager's performance and reputation.[14] The results suggest that city managers are extraordinarily sensitive to and dependent upon favorable council appraisal. For of the fifty-eight managers who responded, forty-two (73%) ranked the council first and an additional thirteen (23%) ranked the council second.

Second, "When role senders are both dependent and powerful," write Kahn and associates, "the situation has about it the pall of hopelessness. The emotional reactions of focal persons to such binding situations reflect this hopelessness."[15] Perhaps the most direct measure of the frequency, intensity, and impact of the policy role conflict can be found in the expressed frustrations of city managers. In field interviews with Bay Area managers, the question was asked: "What would you say are the two most pressing problems or frustrations you face as city manager?" Although responses could run the gamut from community problems to policy matters to personnel questions or to more personal feelings, over 60 percent (25) of the managers identified conflict with the city council as one of their two most important problems or frustrations. Conflict can result from sources other than policy role disagreements; but, upon a rereading of the interview pro-

---

[14]For the exact wording and a commentary on the question of the manager's relative concern for his council, see Chapter four, pp. 61–62.
[15]Kahn et al., *Organizational Stress,* p. 218.

tocols, the main frustration of the managers almost always centers on various aspects of the policy process. For example, here are several illustrative responses:

> The inability to make changes in the interest of efficiency, economy, and progress because of the difficulties in dealing with the lay council. Some councilmen are inept and immature. I am presently dealing with some of that type. They keep putting their noses into my business. I guess this is peculiar to public work, for this type of incompetency is not true in a private corporation. In fact, it is not the best of people on the council. The community could provide a lot better. The job of councilman does not carry much status. This is a big problem for all local communities: how to get highly qualified people to run and serve on the council.

> I find it frustrating that you have a highly trained professional, proficient in efficient and economic operations of city government, subject to the approval of a lay council. A group of men who typically have less education, who are affected by political pressures, who are relatively uninformed, and who invoke personalities, will often reject almost out of hand ideas carefully developed and presented by the manager.

> The council is my number one gripe. When anything goes wrong, I am to blame—it is my judgment, my policies. I am the scapegoat when something goes wrong. . . . The council too often feels it is the expert on everything. Yet, they spend little time in studying problems.

> The first problem would be the city council. Councilmen are not on the council long enough to become oriented into the job, to become aware of the need for open minded evaluation of problems. . . . Councilmen often demonstrate the inability to recognize the long range implications of some of their actions.

> Another frustration is when I think I come up with a real good idea and the staff goes to work on it. Then the council says it doesn't understand—typically without reading reports given to them. What is worse though than not understanding a proposal is the way they are rejected. I don't mind the council not accepting all my ideas but I do object to the casual discussion and study of them.

These conflicts tend to revolve around the unwillingness of the council to accept the policy proposals or leadership of the city manager.

Third—the covert role tension between manager and council is pointed to by the so-called educator function. City managers were asked, "In a research report, I read this quote by a city manager, 'One of the most delicate and important tasks of the city manager is to educate his council without their knowledge.' Do you strongly agree, tend to agree, tend to disagree, or strongly disagree with this statement?" Three out of four managers agreed. The city manager evidently attempts to redefine the values, interests, and expectations of city councilmen. Though indirect, a consensus that supports "indoctrination of the council by the manager" points to salient differences in policy role conceptions as well as how city managers attempt in part to resolve policy role conflicts.

Finally, the managers' version of the ideal councilman again documents the serious character of the policy role conflict. City managers share almost uniform views on "the most important things a city councilman should do." With remarkable unanimity, city managers emphasize legislative and personal traits that spotlight their most important criticisms of city councilmen. A typical indictment, for instance, reads: "The council really shirks its responsibilities; it does not decide issues based on the available information or on community needs. And upon making decisions, the council rarely sells its decisions to the public. Instead, political expediency marks most decisions." To the question "How would you describe the job of being a councilman— that is, what are the most important things a councilman should do?" city managers respond with a profile close to the classical democratic man who is informed, rational, and who decides policy issues in terms of the public interest. A well-known city manager expressed the views of many when he replied:

> A councilman should function as part of the council team, for individually he has no authority whatsoever. He should determine and establish major community goals and provide adequate financing for these goals. He should be well informed and take clear cut

positions on policy proposals. He should act on behalf of the community as a whole, not for some isolated section or special interest. He should ask, what does or will a policy do for the city. Finally, he should devote time to be well informed on policies before he votes or speaks out.

The ideal councilman is a composite of many virtues. One assumption, however, is clearly foremost: he should base his policy decisions on what is good for the community and not on reasons of special interests or political expediency. A councilman should, responds the manager, "get a full picture of the community. He should size up its goals, potential, and problems. The councilman should use this as the focal point to base his evaluation of proposals. Once he has the big picture, he then should try to act fairly objectively within that frame of reference." To this perspective are tied other values. Most often mentioned is the expectation that councilmen should do their homework: "The most important thing is that a councilman should apply himself to the business matters of the city. By application, I mean becoming acquainted with problem areas, appraise alternatives, weigh proposed solutions, and carefully consider his course of action. Too few councilmen really apply themselves." Further, city managers recommend that councilmen be concerned with long-range objectives, willing to take political risks on policy issues, reluctant to interfere in administrative matters, and sensitive to general community demands. City managers on occasion would add also such personal qualities as honesty and intelligence. The normative description emerges that councilmen should be wise tribunes who carefully decide policy questions in terms of the general welfare of the community.

The managers' portrait of the ideal councilman offers a candid description of their conceptions of the proper policy directions and style of city government. The emphasis on the long view and on rational public weal decisions does not, however, find general acceptance among city councilmen. The massive discrepancies between the ideal and real councilmen point to basic differences in policy approaches and views between managers and councilmen. More specifically, the managers' concern with the virtuous

councilman underlines their recognition that what they can do
on policy matters depends to a significant extent on the approval
of their city councilmen.

Consequences of Resolution

The manager faces three choices: (1) he can follow his own
policy definition, (2) he can accept the definition of the council,
or (3) he can engage in some compromise behavior. The third
alternative is the real choice for most managers. The results of
role compromise take myriad forms, with a complex relationship
between policy views and actual behavior in the policy process.
Though difficult to measure, the direction and character of certain
general consequences can be tentatively identified.

First, the city manager cannot act as an elected chief executive
to resolve policy role clashes between himself and the council.
Rather, publicly and to the council, he must present himself as
a professional administrator. Policy activities of any legislative
significance have to be camouflaged or carried out in an informal
and private manner. Thus, the city manager, indirectly or behind
the scenes, strives to build, utilize, and husband his personal
and political resources to influence public policy decisions. To
be successful, he must literally become the best politician in town,
making skillful use of expert, referent, and indirect influence
techniques. Knowledge, reputation, personal ties to outsiders, and
informal contacts with councilmen represent the major access
points to power for a city manager—all of which are for the most
part private, personal, and to a lesser extent professional resources.

Second, the policy questions on which the city manager can
and will expend his political resources are markedly influenced
by the normative perspectives of his council. The result should
have a pronounced impact on the direction and focus of policy
innovation and leadership activities. The overall effect was well
explained in one city manager study as follows:

> Managers were in substantial agreement on the areas where they
> should push hard for managerial policies and the areas where they
> should remain neutral or stay out altogether. They agreed that

managers should assert themselves strongly on technical questions where the best policy is strongly or entirely dependent on factual data. They also strongly defended the responsibility of managers in fields of internal management.

The areas where the managers play a more limited role or stay out altogether include: partisan political issues; moral and regulatory issues; public versus private ownership; the internal operations of the city council; relations with independent boards and commissions and other governments, except as guided by council instructions; and issues where the Council is divided within itself.[16]

The city manager is most likely to act as an innovator and leader in primarily safe areas. But on policy problems of a controversial variety, he is expected by the council to act as staff adviser. In many ways, therefore, the city manager should be a consensus politician par excellence, with high priority given to avoiding friction, criticism, or opposition. Bounded by council sanctions and alert to anticipate their reactions, the city manager cannot initiate or fix priorities or bargain for acceptance of policies as he believes he should. The city manager cannot introduce major policy decisions onto the civic agenda that do not have the implicit approval of the city council, and thus his policy activities are prone to center around particular areas of administrative competence or near community consensus.

Finally, an obvious but often ignored implication is that the city council expects the city manager to participate in policy-making decisions in accord with their wishes and prejudices—and not the abstract values of the public interest or of the city manager profession. When in conflict with the city council, the values of the political executive can be checkmated, neutralized, or temporized. In a study of policy initiation and leadership in three council-manager cities, Charles Adrian concluded, "Questions of timing, social, political, and economic priority, local custom, and even prejudice can and should at times hold precedence over managerial rationale."[17] Because the city council

---

[16]Ridley, *The Role of the City Manager,* p. 39.
[17]Charles Adrian, "A Study of Three Communities," *Public Administration Review,* 18 (1958), 212.

monopolizes most of the important rewards and punishments for city managers, these kinds of questions are likely to be outside the effective purview of most managers. Since role resolution explains much of the dynamics of the policy exchanges between managers and councilmen, these kinds of questions will be treated more extensively in the next chapter.[18]

---

[18]For two excellent statements on the importance and mechanisms of the resolution of role conflict, see Robert Goode, "A Theory of Role Strain," *American Sociological Review*, 25 (August 1960), 483–95; and Robert Merton, *Social Theory and Social Structure* (rev. ed.; Glencoe, Ill.: The Free Press, 1957), pp. 225–386. See also Ronald O. Loveridge, "City Managers in Legislative Politics," *Polity*, 1 (Winter 1968), 213–36.

Chapter 7

City Manager as Policy Maker

Though modest when compared to state and federal activities, the city has jurisdiction over policy areas that profoundly influence the life style of its residents.[1] As a result, city policies cannot be consigned to administrative routines but instead involve the politics of choice—including negotiation, bargaining, conflict, and the mobilization of political support. The kinds of policies a city adopts depend on choices about the allocation of scarce resources and competing values. Thus, despite the hopes of the reform movement, the city manager could not be a neutral participant in the policy process of a city; for he is inextricably involved in the development and execution of policy proposals.

A focus on the city manager as a policy participant invites three questions. First, how does the city manager take part in the policy process? Second, once the outlines of the manager's policy activities can be identified, what is the relationship between policy views and actual participation? That is, do different role perspectives have patterned effects on policy behavior? And, third, how does the city manager resolve the policy differences with his councilmen? More specifically, what policy strategies are employed? And what differences do the contents of a policy

---

[1] See catalog of city functions developed by Oliver Williams and Charles Adrian, *Four Cities* (Philadelphia: University of Pennsylvania Press, 1963), pp. 289-90.

decision make? It is these three questions that this chapter will attempt to answer.

Policy Making: A Comment

The concept of policy making has been loosely interpreted as the initiation, formulation, and presentation of policy matters. For purposes at hand, this crude description requires clarification and sharpening. After a search of the literature, M. Kent Jennings's classification of the policy process was found to be especially useful in analyzing the policy activities of the city manager. The policy process, says Jennings, can be divided into five steps: initiation of action, fixing priorities, utilizing resources for gaining acceptance of chosen alternatives, legitimation, and implementation.[2] This method of classification provides five relatively distinct points at which to examine the city manager and the policy process.

While a policy participant could be a major actor at one stage and unimportant in the next, the city manager has frequent occasion if not the obligation to participate in every stage of the policy process. Exposed and required to do something about the problems of the city, the city manager cannot avoid initiating some kind of policy action. Because of such resources as time, expertise, position, and a near monopoly of technical information about city business, the manager is likely to participate in decisions on how values should be allocated. The same resources again mandate the manager's participation in the promotion of chosen alternatives. As to legitimation, the call for his information, advice, or objections certainly involves the manager in the formal deliberations to decide an issue. And, finally, implementation is the one activity that everyone agrees is the city manager's business; and, as students of public administration tell us, administrators have considerable discretion in interpreting legislation.

---

[2]See M. Kent Jennings, *Community Influentials* (New York: The Free Press, 1964), pp. 107–9.

Two fundamental problems, however, confound this study of the city manager as a policy maker. First, policy making consists of real but largely informal activities that are unfortunately most difficult to identify, measure, or even observe. It involves the recognition of problems and the development of information, a receptive atmosphere, and appropriate persuasion. These activities tend to be of a private character, and thus no public records are available. And, furthermore, the differences between cities play havoc in classifying and comparing policy activities of city managers. A policy issue in one city could be a minor administrative decision in another. How can, for example, the policy activities of the city manager of San Jose (population, 250,000+) be compared to those of the city manager of Los Altos Hills (population, 3,500)?

And, second, a shift in focus from process to policy content offers no satisfactory research strategy. The city is not a blank check on which the city manager can write his policy preferences at will. Rather, the city manager is only one force amidst the situational, structural, and cultural circumstances of a community that determine policy outcomes. No matter what his policy views, skills, or strategies, the city manager can have, at best, only limited effects on most city policies.[3]

For example, though Robert Wood could write in *Suburbia* (1959) that "The city manager tries to formulate policy, sell it,

---

[3]See an excellent essay by Robert Alford on why decisions and policies are adopted. At length, he discusses the possible influence of four independent variables: situational, structural, cultural, and environmental. For example, Alford writes, "The outcomes of particular decision-making struggles over issues will be determined by the pattern of situational factors which exists at the time the decision is made: the incumbents in public office and their political values and skills, the strategic electoral situation, the 'pileup' of issues of various kinds and the bargaining that goes on between interested parties for support, the particular national and state political situation at the given time, the resources which are able to be brought into play by activists, the visibility of the issues to the electorate, the resonance of the issues, against opinions of concerned publics, and many other factors which exist in a particular situation." Alford, "The Comparative Study of the Urban Politics," in *Urban Research and Policy Planning,* Leo Schnore and Henry Fagin, eds. (Beverly Hills, Calif.: Sage Publications, 1967), pp. 263–304.

and if necessary forces decisions distasteful to the city council through the indirect rallying of public opinion,"[4] he found in his *1400 Governments* (1961) that the median income and density of a city are better indicators of the market basket of public goods than any of the conventional political factors. Political sociologists contend that what happens in a city is almost always determined by the numerical and cultural majority of its residents. For that majority is said to support the organizations and institutions that define the city and to form the constituencies to which policy makers are responsive.[5] In other words, despite his skills as a salesman or the urgency of his policy visions, the city manager faces real limits on what policies the council and community will approve or, for that matter, tolerate. These limits imposed by the council and community obscure the linkage between city manager behavior and city policies.

One feasible approach to Bay Area city managers as policy makers is to examine their policy style. That is, what kinds of personal emphases characterize their policy activities? Do they, for example, devote their efforts to administrative operations and routine matters or to policy issues affecting the development of a city? The focus, then, is not the substance of participation but rather the way managers participate in the policy-making process of their city. The assumption is, of course, that the policy style of city managers makes some difference in the direction, perhaps even the fate, of a community.[6]

Policy Behavior: An Overview

The policy style of city managers can ostensibly be studied from data obtained by three research methods: observation, analysis of documents, and interviews. Observation was ruled out, for

---

[4]Robert Wood, *Suburbia* (Boston: Houghton Mifflin, 1958), p. 185.
[5]See, for example, Herbert Gans, *The Levittowners* (New York: Random House, 1967), pp. 408–33.
[6]See William Spinard, "Power in Local Communities," *Social Problems,* 12 (Winter 1965), 335–56.

neither time nor resources were available to observe and record the policy behavior of over fifty managers. Second, the analysis of documents is literally an impossible task—no written records exist for informal policy behavior. Thus, necessity makes a virtue of the third method, asking questions. And no one is in a better position to report policy behavior than the city manager himself. Besides the practical matter that other data are not available, there is a good case to be made that interview responses represent the most accurate source of data on questions of managers' policy style. By asking managers about their routine activities, which center on policy procedures, as well as about nonroutine activities, which focus on innovation and leadership issues, a portrait can be sketched of their policy style.

Routine activities refer to procedural choices faced by city managers. They should indicate whether or not city managers participate as policy executives. Closed questions were used to tap executive behavior in policy matters. (The questions were largely adopted from the Ohio State Leader Behavior Description Questionnaire.[7])

In city legislative politics, city managers participate as policy executives: no other interpretation of Table 7–1 seems possible. City managers are nearly unanimous on six and are highly agreed on ten of the eleven procedural policy choices. There is no reluctance to admit to activities that establish their intimate involvement in the policy process. The city manager participates frequently as a policy initiator, adviser, leader, or spokesman. These results should be expected, for the circumstances that require a city manager's legislative participation have been clearly detailed.[8]

The most crucial policy activities are, however, those that deal with controversial innovation and leadership choices. It is these choices that distinguish the style of the city manager as a policy

[7]See John Hemphill and Alvin Coons, "Development of the Leader Behavior Description Questionnaire," in *Leader Behavior: Its Description and Measurement,* Ralph Stogdill and Alvin Coons, eds. (Columbus: Ohio State University Press, 1957), pp. 6–38.
[8]See Chapter two for an extended discussion of why city managers take part in the city's legislative process.

Table 7–1

Policy Behavior of Managers and Procedural Activities*

	City Managers ($N=40$)		
	Always– Often	Occasionally	Seldom– Never
1. Explain why a particular policy is important	98%	2%	———
2. Make contacts outside of city hall for council	73%	20%	7%
3. Schedule the policies to be taken up	73%	25%	2%
4. Give the council advance notice of policy changes	73%	10%	12%
5. Stand up for council policy even if it is unpopular	98%	2%	———
6. Keep the council well informed on policy matters	98%	———	2%
7. Speak in public in the name of the council	30%	43%	27%
8. Plan ahead on what should be done	98%	2%	———
9. Suggest new approaches to problems	78%	22%	———
10. Keep informed on how councilmen think and feel about policy matters	100%	———	———
11. Back up council members in their policy actions	98%	2%	———

*The procedural questions read as follows: "Here is a list of statements which describe the behavior of individuals in leadership positions. There are five possible answers to each question: always, often, occasionally, seldom, or never. Decide which of the five most closely describes your behavior as city manager." For example, item 1: "I explain why a particular policy is important." Because these questions were not asked in the questionnaire survey, data are from the field interviews with forty city managers. See Appendix A for the entire list of questions.

executive. In order to examine their controversial executive choices, city managers were asked a second sequence of closed questions.[9]

In contrast to responses on procedural activities, city managers report quite dissimilar emphases on nonroutine executive issues (Table 7–2). Some managers opt for a strong, broadly defined participant style, while others are wary, unable, or perhaps unwilling to commit themselves to major innovative or leadership activities. If political power requires a degree of manifest behavior that is intentionally designed to influence the outcome of an issue, some managers emerge as more important participants in the policy process than others. Major differences in policy style thus center on how the manager engages, depends on, or approaches the council and community in terms of nonroutine policy matters.

The city managers' self-portraits as policy makers support two conclusions. First, city managers are active participants in the policy process. Yet, second, the commitment and scope of their policy activities differ noticeably on major issues of innovation and leadership. Managers range from those who resemble political chief executives to others who limit their nonroutine policy activity to informing and advising the council. The point to make

---

[9]The closed questions on controversial executive choices are counterparts of expectation items used to construct manager role types. However, there is a critical distinction. In one, city managers were asked to respond normatively: "A city manager should . . . "; in the other, managers were instructed to describe their actual behavior: "I advocate, maintain, consult. . . ." Thus, although each set asks similar questions, the frame of reference is normative in the first and in the second, behavioral. Possible responses also differ importantly. For the normative set, four responses were available—strongly agree, tend to agree, tend to disagree, and strongly disagree. And for the behavioral items, five possible responses were open—always, often, occasionally, seldom, and never. Admittedly, there is still a question on how independent are the two sets of responses. Managers could perhaps strive for a consistency between normative and behavioral responses that is, in fact, unwarranted. It is nevertheless assumed that varied responses to the closed questions on executive choices are not simply social science artifacts but instead indicate important differences in policy style. That is, a manager who says, "I always advocate major changes in city policies," should display quite different innovative behavior than the manager who replies "never" to the same question.

Table 7–2

Policy Behavior of Managers on Nonroutine Activities*

	City Managers $(N = 40)$		
	Always– Often	Occasionally	Seldom– Never
1. Advocate major changes in city policies	30%	63%	7%
2. Give a helping hand to good councilmen who are coming up for reelection	18%	20%	60%
3. Maintain a neutral stand on any issues on which the community is divided	25%	45%	30%
4. Consult with the council before drafting own budget proposal	15%	18%	65%
5. Assume leadership in shaping municipal policies	47%	38%	15%
6. Encourage people whom you respect to run for the city council	20%	20%	58%
7. Act as an administrator and leave policy matters to the council	41%	33%	22%
8. Advocate policies to which important parts of the community may be hostile	15%	50%	35%
9. Work through the most powerful members of the community to achieve policy objectives	33%	35%	32%

*The nonroutine questions read as follows: "Here are questions on the job of being a city manager: Read each question and then decide which one of the five answers most closely describes what you do here in _____ —do you always, often, occasionally, seldom, or never?" An example, item 1: "I advocate major changes in city policies." For comparative purposes, data again are from field interviews.

is that while all city managers involve themselves in the policy process, their policy style can differ markedly on controversial matters.

Role Perspectives and Policy Behavior

The analysis of policy style raises the second major focus: the relationship of role concepts and behavior. Can differences in policy style be accounted for by the normative views of the city managers? Or in other words, do Political and Administrative managers exhibit patterned differences on nonroutine activities? The payoff of the role typology lies in what it can explain about actual policy-making behavior. If little or nothing, the careful elaboration of manager policy orientations stands as an inconsequential exercise.

One need not expect, however, a one-to-one relationship between role orientations and policy behavior. At most, one might expect general but consistent tendencies in how Political and Administrative managers participate in the policy process. For one, many aspects of policy behavior are more likely to be explained by conditions other than the managers' policy orientations. Policy behavior is clearly constrained and often precipitated by council, city, and circumstantial demands. Also, policy orientations refer to generalized commitments and not a sequence of specific behaviors. Consequently, Political and Administrative orientations should manifest themselves in certain styles or approaches to policy making. These styles may not necessarily take the same form; for no matter what his normative hopes, the city manager has to tailor his policy behavior to the interests, demands, and resources of his community.

When nonroutine activities are analyzed, Political and Administrative managers display strikingly different policy styles (Table 7–3). It would appear that policy orientations are translated in appropriate styles of innovation and leadership on policy matters. With noticeable zeal, Political managers advocate major, often controversial policies and act as good chief executives, politicking

Table 7–3

Policy Orientations and Policy Behavior on Nonroutine Activities: Part One

Nonroutine Activities	Always–Often	Political Managers and Policy Behavior			
		Occasionally	Seldom–Never	Percent	Number
1. Advocate major changes in city policies	50	40	10	100	30
2. Give a helping hand to good councilmen who are coming up for reelection	17	13	70	100	30
3. Maintain a neutral stand on any issues on which the community is divided	10	41	49	100	29
4. Consult with the council before drafting own budget proposal	20	0	80	100	30
5. Assume leadership in shaping municipal policies	72	28	0	100	29
6. Encourage people whom you respect to run for the city council	21	43	36	100	28
7. Act as administrator and leave policy matters to the council	17	24	59	100	29
8. Advocate policies to which important parts of the community may be hostile	25	61	14	100	28
9. Work through the most powerful members of the community to achieve policy objectives	50	27	23	100	30

Table 7-3

Policy Orientations and Policy Behavior on Nonroutine Activities: Part Two

| Nonroutine Activities | Administrative Managers and Policy Behavior | | | | |
	Always–Often	Occasionally	Seldom–Never	Percent	Number
1. Advocate major changes in city policies	18	61	21	100	28
2. Give a helping hand to good councilmen who are coming up for reelection	0	12	88	100	25
3. Maintain a neutral stand on any issues on which the community is divided	37	41	22	100	27
4. Consult with the council before drafting own budget proposal	21	7	72	100	28
5. Assume leadership in shaping municipal policies	32	32	36	100	28
6. Encourage people whom you respect to run for the city council	0	11	89	100	28
7. Act as administrator and leave policy matters to the council	41	29.5	29.5	100	27
8. Advocate policies to which important parts of the community may be hostile	4	35	61	100	28
9. Work through the most powerful members of the community to achieve policy objectives	21	14	65	100	28

for support and endorsement of their favorite policies. In short, they engage in direct and forceful executive behavior on many policy issues.

By contrast, most Administrative managers reveal themselves to be timid policy participants. These managers show a reluctance to make the strong commitments necessary to change the status quo. Some are happy to be administrators, ready to avoid contentious policy questions. Others seem disposed to emphasize the art of the possible. The focus of their major policy efforts is directed more toward administrative than community problems. How a manager defines his policy role would appear to influence the manner in which he uses his position, personal values, and persuasive abilities in the city's policy process.

Further evidence or dissimilar policy styles is provided by the policy recommendations and accomplishments of Political and Administrative managers. How a city manager evaluates and attempts to resolve pressing community problems should reveal his innovative style. For it became obvious in talking with city managers that some wrestle with major problems like urban redevelopment, physical-planning programs, inadequate public facilities, while others adopt a patchwork approach focused on minor policy changes or traditional administrative improvements.

In the field interviews, city managers were asked to identify the two most pressing problems in their community and to indicate what kinds of policies they had or would recommend to solve these problems.[10] Solutions were coded into one of five *scope-of-proposal* categories: major, moderate, piecemeal, unclear, or do-nothing. It merits emphasis that coding decisions were made only after evaluating the relation between policy solutions and the constraints imposed by a community's economic and social char-

---

10The field question on policy recommendations reads, "As you well know, there are always problems in every community. In your opinion, what two problems are most pressing in _____? All right, you noted _____ as a problem. Generally speaking, what have you or will you recommend to the council to meet the _____ problem? O.K. The second problem you noted was _____. Generally speaking, what have you or will you recommend to the council to meet the _____ problem?"

acteristics. To clarify and distinguish their content, selected responses from each of the five categories follow:

MAJOR

Problem—The downtown, the redevelopment of the downtown area. We hope to rehabilitate the downtown area in order to provide a competitive commercial and service environment. The problem is made more difficult because of the growth of regional shopping centers.

Recommendation—We think we are making some progress. After three years of careful negotiating with the Southern Pacific, we have completed a large land agreement. For the right of way through our town we will pay the SP some 10 millions of dollars over a ten-year period. This will provide us with a large piece of land. With the land we can: (1) sell property for off-street parking, and (2) sell strategically located parcels of land for profit. This money will be used to buy other pieces of the SP right of way. Let me give you a specific example. We are building a plaza at the site of the old depot. It will be a town square arrangement with a garden, fountain, and the like. We hope this square will be the focus of the downtown area. While not the geographic center, it is the historic center for the town. The plaza is about to become a reality. New buildings are being built in that area; old ones are being renovated. . . . And the profits we get from sale of land goes into new city buildings. I will discuss this project undoubtedly as the interview progresses. [Plans a new city hall—community center; the design has received national acclaim.]

MODERATE

Problem—First, I think, would be to raise the general standards of community development. This would include the physical plant and aesthetics. Also, we are concerned with the plans for our economic base. We need to strengthen and broaden our economic base. Much of the flat land is residential area. Even what normally could be recreational areas are very limited because of homes. For before the city was incorporated, little thought was given to balancing residential sections with commercial or industrial zones. So we actually now have a very limited area in which to build—at least on desirable land.

Recommendation—To improve our overall community development standards, we have embarked on a number of studies. We have tried to project the economic and social effects of our growing population. Patterns are now set for residential and economic expansion. At the same time, we want to prevent a spiraling of taxes. We have set up architectural controls. All this is an attempt to encourage designs in harmony with the best interests of the city.

PIECEMEAL

Problem—Vehicular traffic!

Recommendation—We are on the way to solving this problem. Soon the John Muir Expressway will be completed. This should be a big help for it will be a thoroughfare through the city. Second, we soon will propose a bond issue to widen Park Road. One obstacle we do have, particularly to secondary thoroughfares, is opposition from homeowners. No one wants heavily traveled streets. We are also improving other intersections to speed traffic.

UNCLEAR

Problem—The first problem would be the capacity of city government to adequately cushion the unprecedented growth and development of an area.

Recommendation—My answer would be twofold: first, to utilize a budget as a program instrument and, second, to set forth community goals and objectives.

DO-NOTHING

Problem—To improve the city's plant facilities, e.g., city hall, corporation yard, etc.

Recommendation—This is a long range goal. Things have not progressed too rapidly. We have a building commission. However, they have not done much—have remained dormant. No bonds are coming up. In truth, the need is there but I have not pushed very hard. Nothing is being pressed. We do, though, have a new fire station and police station. The tempo in our city is slow. Most residents favor the status quo.

Sharp departures are evinced by Political and Administrative managers on matters of innovative style. The differences are most dramatic on major policy proposals, for here only Political managers report such recommendations. Yet, even more important, Table 7–4 indicates that city managers consistently display

Table 7–4

Policy Orientations and Scope of Policy Proposals
on the Two Most Pressing Community Problems

Scope of Proposals	Policy Orientations			Number of Proposals
	Political (N = 21)	Administrative (N = 19)	Percent	
Major	100	0	100	12
Moderate	65	35	100	23
Piecemeal	29	71	100	24
Unclear/Do-Nothing	37	63	100	19

innovative styles that correspond to their policy orientations. Political managers are much more adventuresome and comprehensive in their policy proposals, while Administrators seem often content to keep the city government running smoothly. These differences do not isolate policy nuances but center on some of the most fundamental policy choices made by the manager.

Furthermore, Political and Administrative managers display the same differences on matters of policy leadership. City managers can be characterized by three leadership styles: the community leader, the good government manager, and the status quo administrator.[11] These styles identify differences in the goals, scope, and especially the manner by which city managers attempt to influence the policy process. Community leaders advocate major policy proposals and use what resources they have to exercise community leadership; good government managers center their efforts on improving the service functions of the city and, in turn, realizing the twin goals of efficiency and effectiveness in city government; while status quo administrators work hard to keep city hall running smoothly, emphasizing the procedures of administration rather than the problems of the city. When Political and Administrative managers are classified into one of these three approaches, policy orientations again appear linked

[11]For a similar typology, see Karl Bosworth, "The Manager is a Politician," *Public Administration Review*, 18 (Summer 1958), 216–22.

Table 7-5
Policy Orientation and Three Leadership Styles

Leadership Styles	*Policy Orientations* Political (N = 19)	Administrative (N = 19)	Percent	Number
Community Leader	76	24	100	17
Good Government Manager	43	57	100	14
Status Quo Administrator	0	100	100	7

to differences in policy behavior.[12] Political managers tend to be community leaders, while Administrative managers are almost wholly good government managers or status quo administrators (Table 7-5).

Thus, policy role views account for certain, sometimes significant, differences in policy behavior. How the city manager defines his policy role influences the style of his participation in the policy process. Moreover, the two policy orientations, Political and Administrative, appear to explain why and how city managers take part in city politics. These role perspectives provide standards by which the city manager adjusts and weighs the innumerable policy choices he must make as an appointed executive.

Policy Strategies and Policy Content

Though city managers often act as primary policy makers, they must, at the same time, resolve overt role conflicts with their councils. Despite the admonitions of ICMA spokesmen, city councilmen object to almost all manager activity called policy making. These council attitudes immensely complicate the usual executive choices open to the city manager. The major strategies used by city managers to influence policy decisions can, however, be identified—and merit elaboration.

---

[12]City managers were typed as community leaders, good government managers, and status quo administrators by their responses to a question on past or hoped for policy accomplishments. See Ronald O. Loveridge, "City Managers and Role Analysis" (Ph.D. dissertation, Stanford University, 1965), pp. 251–54.

General Strategies

In practice, common strategies, relevant to any phase of the policy process, are four. Perhaps the favorite is what many managers call "to feel out the situation." If policy making involves the development of information, a receptive atmosphere, and appropriate timing, knowing when and how to participate are vital characteristics. One manager, for example, stressed:

> A city manager has got to have a sense of timing. For he can win battles but lose the war. If a city manager pushes too many programs at once—although they may be needed, he can become a divisive influence. If he uses common sense, he can find out what the council and community would support. By weighing support for programs, progress might take more time but the results will be better. A city manager has to apply temperance.

Repeatedly, managers found reason to point to the art of the possible. Policy should be conceived and fostered within the context of the political values, special interests, and leadership cliques of a city: "A city manager needs a good sense of timing. It is easy to determine what is right. It is much more difficult to develop a sense of political timing." As a prerequisite for influence, city managers must recognize who gets what, when, and how and that controversial policy matters cannot be resolved by administrative fiat.[13]

Second, managers chorus a behind-the-scenes politics, a private approach premised on consulting, advising, and bringing together information and data. Persuasion is accomplished through informal, primarily face-to-face contacts: "The city manager should make recommendations not in public so as to embarrass the council but in private, in caucus sessions, in direct communications, in personal letters." Or, as another manager stated, "The city manager should of course engage in policy making but not openly but tactfully and diplomatically." Managers prefer to be publicly judged and recognized as professional administrators.

---

[13]See Frank Sherwood, "A City Manager Tries to Fire His Police Chief" (Indianapolis: Bobbs-Merrill, Inter-University Case Program #76, 1963) especially pp. 4–5, 8–9.

Concerted efforts are specifically made to place the policy spot-light on the city council.

Third, most managers see education as a fundamental strategy. To convince the council of the wisdom of proposals requires more than ad hoc pleas. City managers instruct councilmen on the complexities and commandments of good government—city manager style. When asked in a research report if "One of the most delicate and important tasks of the city manager is to edu-cate his council without their knowledge," seven out of ten man-agers said they agreed. As one manager replied, "The statement is absolutely true. Especially new councilmen are rank amateurs. I try to teach or better yet inform them as to the total implica-tions of their job, the kinds of problems facing the city. This kind of guidance is essential." The tutorial process takes varied forms; one young manager, for example, responded with this description:

> This area is one which I do in conference and study sessions with councilmen. Occasionally in personnel sessions I give implicit lec-tures. Philosophies are discussed and I try to stress what the ap-propriate roles are. I see that the councilmen get all the proper literature, particularly those pamphlets which the ICMA sends out. Also, I make sure that the council members get to council institutes sponsored by the League.

Almost every manager, whether openly or not, attempts to shape attitudes and perspectives: "I think one of the most important tasks of the city manager is to educate his council. I am not too concerned whether they know it or not. I try to educate them in the best interests of the community." To some extent, every relationship is an implied educational exchange. Yet managers consciously use such exchanges to be more effective policy makers.

Finally, securing the confidence of the council is a fourth strategy. Without the support of the council, the city manager is a weak and vulnerable policy maker. And such support depends on the sustained trust of council members. A young, politically alert manager explained:

> A city manager should gain the confidence of the city council; he should deal with the council as a group; he should avoid creat-

ing the impression of being closer to one segment or the other— councils are generally split; he should understand the individual and collective motivation of the council.

Without the confidence of the council, the manager cannot, quite simply, be an effective policy activist, no matter what tactics are employed. Every manager courts councilmen and avoids policy acts that would provoke their strong suspicion, friction, or opposition: "I do what I can to help them, to encourage them, to make their job easier, to defend their decisions, to carry out their decisions, and to inform them." The city manager has no choice but to maintain a smooth-working relationship with his legislature. And such a relationship only follows from accurate political calculations about the interests and values of the council members.

Specific Strategies

More specific strategies can be examined in terms of the five steps of the policy process: initiation, setting priorities, bargaining, legitimation, and implementation. The first step, initiation, is crucial but exasperatingly complex; for innovative methods are closely tied to situational conditions. Yet, seven strategies could be culled from the city manager interviews; these will be noted along with a word of explanation and an occasional illustration.

1) The manager can introduce important policy changes via the budget. Clarence Ridley reports that all eighty-eight managers he interviewed emphasized that "the budget is the most important method for formulating municipal policy."[14] City managers prepare and propose the budget. Though constrained by past policies, community ideology, and available resources, the manager usually finds that the council makes few changes or objections to his budget proposals.

2) As boss of city hall, the manager can authorize formal reports to raise or dramatize a policy question. A written report

---

[14]Clarence Ridley, *The Role of the City Manager in Policy Formulation* (Chicago: International City Managers' Association, 1958), p. 34.

can carefully document a selected problem and indicate what
can or should be done. The manager can use many reasons to
commission reports. For example, the *Palo Alto Times* recorded
these remarks of the city manager upon his return from a national
conference on natural beauty:

> Keithley listed several major points he plans to study in depth
> with the city staff and City Council: Reexamination of the desir-
> ability of direct burying of underground utility cables. . . . Review
> of signs which are the direct responsibility of the city, including
> their number, organization, and location. The possibility of using
> federal highway funds for freeway beautification. . . . Legislation
> pending approval by Congress which would provide supplementary
> funds to cities might be available for part of the proposed widening
> and beautification of El Camino Real or for downtown improve-
> ments.[15]

3) A corollary and popular strategy is to hire an outside consulting firm to complete a study and make recommendations. In
this way, the manager initiates the policy focus but avoids the
costs of partisan advocacy. For example, one manager candidly
explained, "Let me give you a study I had prepared by a municipal financial consulting firm. No one on this council has seen
this study yet. Its purpose is to prepare the way for a new city
hall and police facilities."

4) The city manager in almost every instance prepares the
council agenda, schedules policies to be taken up, and plans ahead
on what should be done. These privileges allow the city manager
some discretion in raising policy questions. Also, as the funnel
for staff and community proposals, the city manager can further
act as policy gatekeeper for the council and civic agenda.

5) Nonroutine problems such as rapid growth, social conflict,
or falling revenues also permit the manager to exercise notable
policy discretion. These problems can be used to introduce significant policy preferences. For policy change, in a sense, comes
from facing up to new problems: "I am not the sole source for
policy change. For community conditions are changing so rapidly
that new policies by definition have to be made. On a particular

---

[15]*Palo Alto Times,* Thursday, June 3, 1965, p. 24, cols. 3 and 4.

problem, the council expects me to research a change, to present the pros and cons." The manager can thus take the platform of a pressing community problem to propose new or different policies.

6) The city manager can start policy discussions by public use of his staff. For example, many managers now turn to planners to act as advocates for policy changes. In one city, a social-planning coordinator has been hired: "He is conducting an extensive study of the city, looking into problems of population, income, delinquency, etc. We are attempting to get the real picture—then set up projects." Other managers rely on the professional expertise of the planner to initiate new directions in policy development: "We want to improve the environment . . . to upgrade the life style here; we have hired a very active and very capable planner—he is one of the best around." And still others use the master plan.

7) Finally, informal suggestions can be an invaluable method for placing a policy idea on the civic agenda. Suggestions are frequently made to councilmen and even occasionally to community influentials. "Some managers," writes Ridley, "have found that they can successfully instigate action on policy by suggesting programs either to the mayor or to individual members of the council and thus encourage them to 'carry the ball' in decision making." The face-to-face small group character of city politics encourages a less formal initiation process than exists at the state or national levels.

After initiation, the policy process becomes crowded with participants. To influence the content and support of policy proposals, the manager has, nonetheless, recourse to various strategies. One strategy centers in the relations between manager and council. Managers know councils work with the information and recommendations they supply. The manager can exercise some discretion from research to recommendations: for example, "The council expects me to give recommendations. I give alternatives —however, I usually weigh the alternatives" or "The council expects me to a large extent to make recommendations. In fact, there is a dependence on the city manager for recommendations, both publicly and privately. And these recommendations can take subtle forms." Many managers, moreover, act on the assumption that they should have a direct influence:

> How do you remain neutral about policies that affect the operation of the city. The city develops slowly. The staff tries to point out the continuities in policy, how a policy is part of a cohesive whole. There are no areas which I stay out of that influence the character of the city. The fellow who says, "I sit in my office and the council lets me know what I should do," is a secretary, not a city manager.

Advocacy can also take other forms. A common approach is to credit councilmen with originating a proposal and then champion the cause. The manager can here take an open course of leadership but attribute innovation to the wishes of his councilmen.

Beyond the council chambers, managers frequently use more political strategies. The most obvious is to bargain and negotiate for agreement on policy issues. At times, the focus is still the council: "I see the city manager's role as a catalyst, a unifier. Before meetings, I have to do considerable work in the background, over drinks, on the telephone, in private and semi-private meetings. All this is necessary to get some sort of agreement at council meetings." On other occasions, managers work with the leadership of important groups. As one veteran manager observed, "You have to have a collection of publics behind a major proposal." City managers also speak readily about working with community influentials:

> In a city, I look for the opinion makers rather than groups. In every city there is a small number of men and women who influence public opinion. They are usually vocal and respected, although not necessarily liked. Many times they are associated with the newspaper or particular prestigious organizations. The people of the town listen to these opinion makers. Success comes to a city manager who can convince the opinion makers that a project is good for the city.

Whether for reasons of fixing priorities, coalescing support or co-opting opposition, city managers cannot limit their politicking to city hall. For example, managers often encourage special interest groups to provide the political force for a policy proposal. Downtown business groups are especially likely recruits as sponsors: "For public parking plazas in the downtown area, we worked closely with the Chamber of Commerce. We relied on them to stir up the interest." Finally, the city manager through community contacts and, more importantly, the press can summon public attention and pressure to bear on crucial community issues. Subtle in form, what the manager and staff think has a definite influence on the public dialogue on major policy questions. Many good government groups, for instance, view the manager's perspective and the public interest as one and the same.[16]

Implementation, the final step, offers two fundamental policy strategies. Public administration students stress the discretion possible in administering policy decisions. The administrator invokes his own values and interests as a policy decision is translated from the general to the specific. However, the visible and personal character of local politics makes any major departures from council intent a dangerous course. On the other hand, managers can exercise discretion in what problems are brought to the attention of the council: "After finding out what he can do and what he can't do, the city manager should make all the decisions he can without going to the council." Over time, the city manager and his staff can make a number of decisions that commit the city to major policies—often without the recognition or expressed approval of the council. A very successful city manager explained the strategy in these words:

> Major policy decisions are made by the council. Administrative policy is set by the city manager. And we set an awful lot of policies. Before bringing a policy before the council, we ask ourselves whether it is an administrative policy—and this you might say is a flexible criterion.

Participation for What?

The rules of the local policy process require that city managers participate; yet these managers can exercise marked discretion on what kinds of issues they will use their repertoire of policy

---

[16]Wood quotes one city manager who expressed the point more directly, "God bless all civic associations. They are the city manager's ward machines." See Wood, *Suburbia,* pp. 184, 175–86; also Leonard Goodall, *The American Metropolis* (Columbus, Ohio: Charles Merrill, 1968), pp. 59–64, for a similar viewpoint.

strategy. For example, a city manager can focus his policy resources largely on bureaucratic effectiveness and efficiency or on the enlargement of the goals and functions of the city. When asked on what policy areas they "pushed hard" or "remained neutral or stayed out," most managers took the occasion to distinguish among policy areas. Almost three out of four replied that they pushed hard on administrative matters or issues related to the office of the city manager: "I push hard on policy matters which affect the administrative machinery, the operations of city services. I would not push hard on items that are outside of that realm." But as the last remarks suggest, when policy areas become less technical or financial and more political, city managers are noticeably less willing to do battle.

To illustrate, managers can be classified into one of five levels of activity, a hierarchy of policy involvement from those who push hard in all areas to those who push hard in no areas. The levels represent differences in uses of resources to influence policy decisions, with costs greater in time and energy and commitment for the higher levels (Table 7–6).

1) *Push hard in all or at least the most important areas:* I will stay out of a policy matter if it is insignificant as far as the city is concerned. For example, we now have a controversy going over fluoridation of a part of the city's water service. Normally, I would stay out of something like this. While I think I would be in favor, there is no real reason why I should get involved. On major policy and planning decisions or proposals, I am involved. I gauge the importance of a policy before deciding to enter.

2) *Push hard where community goals and objectives are at stake:* I stay out of issues which involve politics—of course, I guess all issues involve politics in one form or another. More precisely, I stay out of areas based upon different personality viewpoints. I push hard in areas of development and land use policy. I also push hard on financial policies. In personnel matters, I tend to remain more or less neutral.

3) *Push hard on administrative matters and technical questions:* Policies that are technical in nature or have to do with administrative matters, I push hard. . . . Policies in a political area or that have to do with political, moral, or spiritual questions, I usually keep hands off entirely.

Table 7–6
Highest Level of Manager Policy Participation*

Level of Policy Activities	Percentage Saying "Push Hard" (N = 36)
All–Most Policy Areas	14
Community Goals	25
Administrative Areas	36
Council Objectives	14
No Area	11
	100

*For each manager, the highest level of policy commitment was recorded.

> 4) *Push hard in policy matters only when so indicated or endorsed by the city council:* It depends on what the situation is. What you do depends on your working relationship with the council. Sometimes they expect you to push hard.

> 5) *Push hard in no area:* I think these people do not want to be pushed hard on anything. They don't mind not deciding a question. In fact, they would like to slow down the rush of local government. I have learned never to say that we must have this decided tonight.

Though a frequent policy participant, the occasion for conscious intervention of the manager varies importantly. Managers subscribe to different objectives for their policy involvement; and, in turn, these differences should influence a city's priorities and decisions on policy. Those managers who extend their policy interests beyond city hall are more likely to effect a sense of direction, style, and content to civic life. Almost every manager identified by three or more colleagues as outstanding can be found in the first two levels of involvement. They tend to "push hard on programs to improve the city" in terms of a vision of making the community a better place to live and work. These accomplishments necessarily depend on the political strategies of the manager and the willingness of his council to approve new proposals. The major obstacles center on the refusal of the city council to endorse such policy activities. And the more publicly contested the issue, the more vulnerable the manager becomes to council prejudices and demands.

Chapter 8

City Manager in Community Politics

Though conceived and structured on the dichotomy between politics and administration, the city manager is now required to meet political problems never envisioned by early proponents of the plan. The near radical change in the raison d'être of the city manager requires us to ask what are the policy values of the manager? What happens to these values in practice? What difference can a city manager make? And what are the future prospects of the city manager? While these questions are subtle and complex, this study of Bay Area city managers presents an excellent departure for analysis, evaluation, and speculation.

Policy Role Reexamined

Shift in Ideology

For the last fifty years, the policy role of the city manager has been a frequent and worthy focus of controversy. The controversy goes to the basics of city government: what should the city manager be about? Preferences for one policy role or another are, in essence, answers to the question of city government for what? Put briefly, a decisive ideological shift has occurred. The initial limited conception of city government with its emphasis on neutral competence has been replaced by a more positive view of city government and a concern with executive leadership among city managers. Though proponents of the housekeeping perspective occasionally make an appearance, the values of executive leadership—in some form or another—are now dominant.[1] Advocacy and agreement on an aggressive policy role orientation can be almost uniformly found in the recent academic and professional literature on local government.

The change in policy role emphasis from neutral competence to executive leadership is not unique to city managers. Rather, this shift follows a more general development among almost all political executives. The reasons are familiar and said to apply to all levels of government. Yet the city manager presents an interesting case because he is the one chief executive who is at the beck and call of his legislature. Moreover, the legal and symbolic traditions of the council-manager plan prohibit executive leadership by the manager. In this context, let us briefly examine four explanations of why the city manager's policy role has been redefined.[2]

1) Functional requirements—The city manager runs city hall. With a part-time council forbidden by statute from interfering in administration, the city manager has a near monopoly on information. As a result, he literally cannot avoid close involvement in the policy-making process. Likewise, success as a city manager will depend more on the handling of policy problems than his technical management of city operations. Whether by choice or not, the city manager has had to assume some political leadership. Banfield and Wilson agree that "Probably the functional requirements of the plan, and not the 'good government' ideology behind it, account for the political aspects of the manager's role."[3]

2) Professional values—City managers share common goals not identified by the official orthodoxy of the Model City Charter of

[1]Strong objections to executive leadership still come, however, from city councilmen. City councilmen, as discussed earlier, prefer the city manager to deal primarily with administrative matters and leave policy matters to the council.
[2]For a careful, though sometimes one-sided, critique of Richard Childs' conception of the policy and political role of the city manager, see John East, *Council-Manager Government: The Political Thought of Its Founder, Richard S. Childs* (Chapel Hill: University of North Carolina Press, 1965).
[3]Edward Banfield and James Q. Wilson, *City Politics* (Cambridge, Mass.: Harvard University Press, 1963), p. 176.

the National Municipal League. In *Four Cities,* Oliver Williams and Charles Adrian conclude, "But the manager is not simply an administrator, for his profession incorporates a sense of mission. The city manager's code of ethics asserts that 'The city manager . . . has a constructive, creative, and practical attitude toward urban problems and a deep sense of his own social responsibility as a trusted public servant.' Thus the manager is a problem-solver by trade."[4] Reputation and success of the manager are tied to concrete achievements. Professional values thus further encourage the city manager to participate decisively in the public policy process. For the kudos of the profession go to those managers who have effected a sense of direction, style, and content to civic life. And it is these accomplishments that are the distinguishing criteria of excellence of the city manager profession.[5]

3) Urban complexities—The conflict between expertise and authority is a theme central to modern decision making. Marked disparities exist between manager and councilmen on matters of information and technical skills. The city manager for one is required to put together and interpret information from many specialized sources. And as a trained, full-time practitioner, the manager is in a position to develop an understanding of city problems that individual councilmen find all but impossible to rival. The city manager thus enters the policy process with the "black box" expertise of local government at his command. Now introduce the increasingly complex nature of city problems, and the third reason for the manager's participation becomes clear. Problems are such that almost no one else can be as knowledgeable about their meanings, consequences, and possible solutions; as Iola Hessler explains:

> The increasing complexity of urban problems, the rapid rate of change in the kinds of services demanded by cities, the growing dependence of government upon "experts," the mushrooming growth of electronic data processing, and the developing impact of

---

[4]Oliver Williams and Charles Adrian, *Four Cities* (Philadelphia: University of Pennsylvania Press, 1963), p. 283.
[5]See Ronald O. Loveridge, "Ten Top Managers in the San Francisco Bay Area," dittoed paper, University of California, Riverside (1965).

federal subsidies and controls on local governments, all require an intensification of the use of the professional in city government.[6]

4) New demands—Early reformers hoped the city would become an impartial clearinghouse for a limited set of goods and services. Good government was to be efficient, economical, and honest administration: the message was administration, not politics. Accelerating changes in technology, population, ecology, life styles, and race relations pose policy issues that the city manager must confront. As one manager observed:

> The whole concept of the city manager's position, functions, and role in the city has and is changing. Originally the idea was that the manager (and the council-manager form) were for the purpose of correcting waste, inefficiency and to bring order and coordination to city operations. This then was the manager's function and primary job. That job has now been done (we hope) and efficiency and economy are by-products taken for granted. The manager's primary functions have moved on to other areas involved in planning, discernment of trends and changing conditions and proposing changes, shifts or new functions to keep in step with the times, governmental relations, etc.

Views of the City Manager

The ideological shift from neutral competence to executive leadership is readily expressed by city managers. They articulate a policy orientation close to the values of the political executive. The interview results from Bay Area managers permit no other conclusion. These managers reject first the dichotomy between politics and administration; for they see participation in the policy process as required and, more important, necessary. And beyond participation, managers do not view their policy goals as those of scientific management but instead those directed toward policy formulation, program development, and other broad aspects of governing a city. While the policy role allows no exact or universal definition, most city managers self-consciously com-

---

[6]Iola Hessler, *29 Ways to Govern a City* (Cincinnati: Hamilton County Research Foundation, 1966), p. 96.

mit themselves to innovation and leadership in the policy process.[7]

Yet all managers do not share the same general policy orientation. Some still define the policy role within a fairly narrow context, stressing housekeeping and not policy decisions. Almost
without exception, however, these managers can be explained by
two related scenarios. The first is the manager of the small town
(population less than ten thousand). Many of these cities are
upper middle-class preserves where the manager acts as caretaker;
the tenor is well illustrated by a verse recited by one such manager:

> We thank the Lord for all thy grace
> In bringing us to this lovely place
> And now dear Lord we hopefully pray
> Thou will keep all other folks away.

The manager is hired to conserve and protect the living space of
its well-to-do residents. One successful manager of a large city
referred to these men as overpaid subdivision marshals. Tied also
to size is complexity of city government. In small cities, the manager is faced with almost no staff and many routine, operational
tasks. To this point, a young manager in a city of less than five
thousand people lamented, "Probably as much as 40 hours a
week I would not do what I am doing here if I were in a larger
city." The small city manager, without choice, has to devote much
of his time to work as a technician. Thus, the values and activities
of a small city can result in the recruitment of managers with an
orientation to neutral competence.

The second scenario takes place in the life history of the manager. Access to the city manager profession is wide open, limited
only by the discretion of city councils. Entry does not depend
upon certification or special training. Bay Area managers range
in education, for example, from those with advanced degrees in
law or public administration to several who did not complete
high school. Certain recruitment and career patterns, however,
are now pronounced. And it is the exceptions to these patterns
that make up most of the managers who express a weak policy

---

[7]See Chapter four, especially pp. 48–51.

orientation. That is, managers appointed without a college education, an engineering background, little or no career experience, a lack of interest in the professional game, or an anti-government philosophy are likely to prefer a passive and limited policy role orientation. Even more than a small city, these kinds of career experiences and goals—or their opposites—appear to influence how the manager will define his policy role.

Though access remains unregulated, city managers increasingly share a common sequence of career choices and experiences. Most managers—and especially those younger than forty—are likely to be trained and tested public executives. These men see themselves as city hall generalists, obligated to take an active part in the public process. They now recognize that past virtues are not good enough; as one manager recently observed, "The chief challenge to council-manager government is to match the needs of the current social change in urban America. Cities are for people and the emphasis should now be on improving service to people. Training and education should be for the purpose of equipping managers to fill their new roles as community leaders and as mediators between employee groups, citizen groups, citizens, and city hall. Greater emphasis must be made on social problems and the development of administrative policy in social fields."

Views of the City Councilmen

By contrast, the ideological ferment over the place of the city manager has not importantly penetrated the ranks of city councilmen. The formal myths and rituals of good government are largely accepted and approved, with its conventional wisdom providing the prism through which city managers are evaluated and exhorted. Bay Area city councilmen overwhelmingly endorse the conception of the manager as a staff adviser hired to give advice and information on city affairs as well as to administer policy passed by the council.[8] The values of neutral competence, not executive leadership, are the orthodox views of city councilmen. For most councilmen have agreed upon the policy image of the city manager as a staff administrator as opposed to a political executive.

---

[8]See Chapter five, especially pp. 80–84.

The council conception of city manager as staff adviser cannot be overemphasized. Despite telling criticisms and new circumstances, the formal separation of administration and politics is still a major article of faith. City councilmen strongly object to the manager as a policy inventor or community leader: in brief, policy advocacy is not sanctioned. For example, when Bay Area city councilmen were asked to check who initiates policy matters, the refusal to credit the manager as a major policy innovator was evident:

Initiation of Policy Matters	N = 293
Manager initiates all policy matters	1%
Manager initiates most policy matters	9%
Manager and council equally initiate policy matters	31%
Council initiates most policy matters	25%
Council initiates all policy matters	33%

The symbolic policy prerogatives written into the council-manager plan are believed, defended, and thought to be acted upon. Councilmen are unwilling to grant the city manager much in the way of an open and independent policy position.

Tension and Conflict

The policy role defines the manager's purposive identity as a chief executive. As such, it becomes the focus of conflict over the manager's role. While managers, because of training, functions, and circumstances, have adopted an executive orientation, they are required to reconcile and resolve such values with the often strong objections of councilmen. The result is an ad hoc, uncertain game of policy advocacy, played out in the very personal executive-legislative exchanges of council-manager politics. Though success for the manager depends on concrete results, his first priority is to survive. And to survive means to practice the art of the possible with his city council.[9]

---

[9]See Chapter six, especially pp. 102–8.

It is true that frustration is rampant among all urban executives and that a massive gap exists between what they feel they should do and what they can do. "The decisive feature," writes Leonard Reissman, "of the practitioner's position is an almost complete lack of power to affect urban trends in any significant way. Confronted most of the time by the consequences of previously unplanned actions, he is further restricted to a narrow range of possible steps he can take to solve the problems they have raised. It is not that he lacks judgment or knowledge; he lacks the means to do almost anything of positive and lasting consequence."[10] Nevertheless, the manager faces a unique problem. His council, the significant other, exercises the power to hire and fire and, more importantly, it holds an abiding wariness of the manager's policy activities and a jealous preference for its own privileges and outlook. No other major American political executive has to deal with the question of legislative supremacy. The interpretation of the policy role is probably the predominant source of stress for the manager. Unlike other professionals, the manager is punished and rewarded not by his peers or by formal criteria but by a group of part time amateurs.

Ideology and Performance

Role Expectations and Policy Behavior

The celebrated shift from neutral competence to executive leadership becomes important primarily because role expectations are assumed to influence role behavior. That is, policy role orientations are thought to provide values and meanings that significantly influence policy behavior. To paraphrase Heinz Eulau, people behave in terms of the meaning they give politics.[11]

---

[10]Leonard Reissman, *The Urban Process* (New York: The Free Press, 1964), pp. 28–29.

[11]Heinz Eulau, *Behavioral Persuasion in Politics* (New York: Random House, 1963), p. 6. The quotation has been modified; it correctly reads, "And the meanings that people give to politics are appropriate data for scientific analysis because people behave in terms of these meanings." See discussion of cultural context (pp. 62–84) for further elaboration of this position.

The definition of the policy role identifies a rough yet consistent sociopolitical road map for most city managers. For it represents, in a real sense, the city manager's attempt to structure his social reality, to define his place within it, and to guide his search for meaning and gratification.

Yet the linkage between attitudes and behavior is complex. No one disputes that policy expectations exercise some influence on policy behavior, but the question of how much is a matter of controversy. The scholar who sets out on such a venture faces a long and troublesome list of empirical and theoretical difficulties. The city manager, besides normative expectations, acts and reacts to a vast variety of other personal and situational variables. Moreover, even policy orientations have a given set of latitude, allowing certain options and disallowing others, with varying degrees of clarity and strictness. Concrete behavior should thus be diversified, constant only in its general character. As observed by the authors of *The Legislative System*, "Role theory helps us to predict certain general types of responses."[12]

The study of Bay Area city managers nevertheless does show that major similarities and differences in policy behavior can be partly explained by role orientations. If the responses of managers can be accepted as accurate, their policy values are consistently translated into the practice of city management. Especially on nonroutine questions of innovation and leadership, the policy styles of city managers appear clearly influenced by their role orientations. The normative political road map of the city manager thus does make a difference in how he will use his position to initiate and promote policy objectives.[13]

Policy Goals and Values

If he is a community leader, for what ends does the city manager take part in community decisions? Robert Wood says, "What the suburbanite wants above all is an efficient, economical, honest,

---

12John Wahlke, Heinz Eulau, William Buchanan, and LeRoy Ferguson, *The Legislative System* (New York: John Wiley & Sons, 1962), p. 20.
13See Chapter seven, especially pp. 119–26.

conservative government that gives him the services he wants when he wants them, at less cost than he would have to pay in the core city."[14] Are these also the objectives of the city manager?

At the most personal level, the prime objective of almost every manager is to survive. Without the continuous advice and consent of the city council—a difficult thing to obtain in many cities— the city manager can look forward only to meager accomplishments and early dismissal. Thus the constant need of, and concern with, council approval conditions the policy objectives pursued by the city manager.

Yet beyond survival, the major innovative and leadership objectives of city managers require comment. To what vision of the good city do city managers direct their efforts? What priorities furnish the political criteria for nonroutine decisions? These and related questions present puzzles that defy exact answers. In general, Bay Area managers cited their most important policy accomplishments in three areas: administrative efficiency and effectiveness, bricks and mortar results, and community destiny decisions.[15] For some managers, the economical provision of goods and services is their central policy creed. Others go beyond the housekeeping activities of city hall to emphasize the capital expenditures of the city, taking special pride in city building programs. And a third group of managers focuses more on the development of the city's public and private life style.

To be more specific, let us examine the policy goals of four of the top five city managers in the Bay Area. The verdict of professional success was provided by responses to this question:

> In the nine counties making up the Bay Region (Alameda, Contra Costa, Marin, Napa, San Mateo, Solano, Sonoma, San Francisco, and Santa Clara), whom do you regard as the five most outstanding city managers? Please write in five names.

The top five managers were those who received the most nominations from their colleagues. These managers serve to illustrate the policy values that guide manager participation in community

---

[14]Robert Wood, *Suburbia* (Boston: Houghton Mifflin, 1958), p. 153.
[15]See Chapter four, especially pp. 73–77.

decisions; for they should express the predominant standards for their profession.[16] Moreover, they act as models as well as spokesmen for other managers—and especially new recruits. As such, the policy objectives voiced by four outstanding managers stand as crucial yardsticks of what policy differences city managers hope to make.

Manager A, highly regarded, with a national reputation, is a quiet-spoken, pipe-smoking, middle-aged man. The city manager in the same city for sixteen years, Manager A has been a major participant in the development of its physical structure and political ethos. He explained his general view of the policy objectives of a manager in these words, "to keep things on an even keel, to implement a long range plan, and to make the community a good place to live and work in." Yet Manager A is also quick to moderate his own powers and values: "A city manager should not get the idea that he works for the general public— you work for the council. Councilmen are the bosses. What a city manager does in policy matters depends on the structure of the council and the community. There is no one set rule. A city manager, however, has to do things no one else will do; and usually it is the manager whether he likes it or not who gets involved in policy leadership." Though his vision of the good city is modified by what is possible, Manager A insists on the place of the manager in influencing if not effecting community destiny decisions—"I push hard on long range plans and proposals." This position of advocate for long-range developments or improvements is a clear thread interwoven through much of the interview.

Manager B, a tall, distinguished-looking man in his early fifties, displays a blunt, impatient manner and a tough, exacting intelligence. A veteran manager of a middle-size city, Manager B has been remarkably successful in making his city an example par excellence of an All-American city.[17] The manager, he be-

---

[16]As George Floro explains, managers who are judged by colleagues to be outstanding provide the ideals and act as custodians of the professional heritage. See George Floro, "Continuity in City-Manager Careers," *American Journal of Sociology*, 61 (November 1955), 240–46.

[17]The city was chosen by a national news magazine as one of the fourteen best American cities in which to live, shop, and work.

lieves, should be a decisive political participant in the policy process:

> A city manager can determine and form policy; he particularly should do so when he thinks it is essential to the community. If he feels the results would be bad, by all means he should involve himself. In making policy, however, the city manager should not make the council feel that he is infringing on their powers. And he should not put the council on the hot seat.

Manager B seems to have no explicit program for when he will take an active part, but rather says it depends on his interpretation of the consequences or importance of a policy issue: "If policy is of little consequence, I stay out. Whether or not we should have dog leashes is a good example. If a policy is important or I have recommended it, I get involved." While willing to cite specific accomplishments such as building up a good staff and strong tax base, Manager B's policy concerns focused on nonroutine community decisions, especially those of long-range purpose and direction. As he explained, "I think our number one problem is deciding where we go from here. It is not a question of master plans. We have plans galore. We have reports by planners, consulting outfits, and the like. The problem is not locating objectives but instead arriving at a consensus." Moreover, he further pointed to the inability of the city to remain isolated from problems of change, for example, traffic and race. These comments should put into clear focus Manager B's concern with the future of the community and how he can encourage and achieve a consensus for private and public action.

Manager C, a friendly, perceptive manager in his late forties, has advanced to the top by moving from city to city. Unlike the first two, he manages a city that has experienced few recent changes, in population or otherwise. As he indicated, "We are really a reactionary community. The populace doesn't want to do anything; they want everything to remain the same." Frustrated by a lack of civic leadership or imagination, he feels he should exercise strong but private leadership on community issues of importance and on which some impact is possible. More generally, Manager C also believes the manager should be an active but faceless policy maker:

> The real distinction is what you should not do publicly in contrast to what you must do privately. A city manager should be more than a council adviser. He should urge and recommend policy. He should write policies for others to present. . . . But he should not lead publicly. I think a city manager should be a faceless man in the community; he should not be widely known. This is not only safe but practical. All credit should go to the council. If a city manager accepts credit, then he must also accept blame.

The precise policy objectives for which the manager should work are again tied to circumstances. Yet he argues for real and major changes: "I have master plans coming out of my ears. It is frustrating to me to see what could be done and what we are doing. This does not sound very democratic, but when I see a problem where the solution is obvious, I think something ought to be done. Instead, long, arduous preparation is necessary to even make an attempt." The tenor of Manager C's remarks reveals a striking frustration with the inability to influence significant community destiny decisions. His concerns are not efficiency and economy or new capital expenditures but rather a renovation of the city's design and political style. The policy goals he proposes are not those of the residents but of the management profession; he wants a city to move and adapt to changing conditions and new options of the modern emerging city.

Manager D, long-time manager of the same city, is a short, friendly man in his middle fifties. In his tenure as manager, the city has developed from modest size to a large, sprawling urban metropolis. Manager D places emphasis on community growth and not on the mechanics of administering city hall. For example, long-range planning and redevelopment projects are his choices for the two most pressing city problems. He advocates full and direct involvement of the manager in the policy process:

> The city manager has to administer the city. But more than that, he should set forth strong recommendations to his council on all matters of policy which have to do with the welfare of the city. And he should attempt to sell diligently his recommendations.

Further, much as an elected chief executive, he says the city manager has to meet with and seek the support of interested community groups. Like the other three, Manager D asks what the consequences and importance of a policy issue are before he decides to participate—"I will stay out of a policy matter if it is insignificant as far as the city is concerned. . . . On major policy and planning decisions or proposals, I am involved. I gauge the importance of a policy before deciding to enter." Perhaps a better clarification of his policy objectives can be found in his list of personal accomplishments:

> First, I would say the most important accomplishment has been to keep up with and in many respects ahead of the city's growth. This includes maintaining such services as libraries, parks, sewer treatment, storm drainage, fire houses, etc. . . . Second, we have been among the leaders in the approach to racial matters. We set up a Social Relations Commission—the first in the state. Third, we have set up long range community development programs, especially for capital investments. Fourth, we have been among the first in the nation to pioneer the sister city ideal. And fifth, we have built the city aggressively. From 17 square miles, we expect to become one of the largest cities in northern California, both in area and in population.

These are notably balanced objectives: the provision of goods and services; management of conflict; and a commitment to the American virtues of size, progress, and the future.

The four managers, at the top of the profession in visibility and prestige, lay claim to an aggressive, almost visionary, policy role. Policy concerns, while tempered by pragmatic restraint, are focused on the good life and general welfare of the city.[18] Rejecting the dichotomy between politics and administration, the four choose to enter the policy process to influence major community decisions. They are not pro-business in their social values or conservative in political outlook; instead, the four articulate

---

[18]For similar findings, see Lloyd Wells' study of twenty-six city managers in the state of Missouri. Lloyd Wells, "Social Values and Political Orientations of City Managers: A Survey Report," *Southwestern Social Science Quarterly,* 48 (December 1967), 443–50.

and work for what has been called a Community Conservationist ideology. The Community Conservationist, Robert Agger and colleagues explain, "believes in a public interest that may differ from the shortsighted, limited interest of a portion of the community, stresses the need for and the duty of the government to provide long-range planning in the public interest by nonpolitical administrators. . . . Cultural values are such that the programs of civic improvement and repair which they favor tend to make them advocates of vigorous, expansionist government. These programs include a stress on the improved distribution of knowledge through the public schools, cleanliness and beauty in architecture, planning a guided development of land use and of the size and character of the community's population, and a spirit of harmonious cooperation on the part of the citizenry."[19] The four managers, in other words, place heavy emphasis on meeting the problems brought to the civic agenda by change and the development of community life style and civic identity. They thus share a futuristic orientation to public service directed toward a balanced, integrated city.

Prerogatives and Strategies

To influence policy decisions, city managers can draw on a fluctuating supply of prerogatives and strategies. City managers have successfully used these resources to shape policy outcomes. Yet what a specific manager can do on a specific decision depends, of course, on a complex mixture of opinions and circumstances. However, several crucial differences in the impact of the city manager can be demonstrated by a typology of policy decisions: routine and nonroutine administrative decisions and routine and nonroutine community decisions. (Administrative decisions are distinguished from community decisions by the personal control and discretion available to the manager, while routine decisions are distinguished from nonroutine decisions by the kind of com-

---

[19]Robert Agger, Daniel Goldrich, and Bert Swanson, *The Rulers and the Ruled* (New York: John Wiley & Sons, 1964), pp. 25, 29.

munity consensus and controversy that is associated with a policy issue.[20])

Administrative decisions—On routine administrative decisions, for example, hiring a new clerk or setting up a new accounting procedure, the city manager in large measure can make the decision himself. From initiation to implementation, few obstacles, except office politics and available resources, present themselves. In the day-to-day running of city hall, the city manager is his own master. Discretion is such that no major political strategies are required to exercise his own will. By contrast, on nonroutine administrative decisions, for example, building a new city hall or firing a well-liked police chief, the city manager has to use what resources he has to bargain with and persuade others. Often a working consensus will depend on the political skills of the manager. Though he can initiate, inform, and ultimately implement a decision, the problems of fixing priorities, gaining acceptance, and achieving legitimation call for various strategies. Nevertheless, the city manager is in a position to engage the policy process, to play a major role in how and what is decided. Even nonroutine administrative issues are largely concerned with questions on which the city manager has the most information and can quite properly bring his prestige and reputation to bear. Within limits set by the council and community, the city manager should have considerable political influence on nonroutine administrative issues.

Community decisions—On routine matters, for example, attracting a new department store or sponsoring a sister-city program, the city manager can and often will participate. Given his reputation, information, and contacts, he can readily enter the policy process on issues where community consensus exists. Despite the fact that routine community decisions are outside of the administrative rulebook for the manager, few objections are raised if widespread agreement exists. With careful use of available

---

[20]The distinction between routine and nonroutine decisions was suggested and adapted from M. Kent Jennings, *Community Influentials* (New York: The Free Press, 1964), pp. 107–54.

resources, the city manager can frequently originate and gain acceptance for many kinds of routine community decisions.

Finally, on controversial community decisions—for example, low-cost housing, jobs for the unemployed, urban renewal—the city manager must exercise enormous care in how he participates. As a professional, he can advise and suggest, but where a consensus does not exist, he has to make his case in private and not openly differ from the interests and values of the city council or a majority of community influentials. Yet achieving community consensus on sociopolitical solutions presents major challenges to the city manager, as Desmond Anderson explains:

> The very nature of the role of the urban manager is such that he is clothed with responsibility for innovation and change. . . . His role as change agent is brought into stark relief when viewed against public opinion which, once solidified, is stubbornly resistant to change. In the process of focusing or aiding in the focus of opinion on public policy issues, participating in policy determination, implementing a favorable program, and overcoming resistance to change in each phase of a continuing process, the manager is operating as a community leader.[21]

Policy Strengths and Weaknesses

The policy successes and failures of the city manager pose evaluative questions that survey data from Bay Area managers cannot answer. Nevertheless, the review and analysis of manager-council relations suggest several observations. First, the popular goals of the early reformers—efficiency, impartiality, and honesty —have largely been met. Due to personal discretion and a pivotal location, city managers can make or influence most administrative decisions; and to these decisions, managers have brought managerial expertise, a commitment to public service, and a professional code of ethics. In *City Politics,* Banfield and Wilson write, "although there is no way of proving it, we suspect that the council-manager plan has been a cause as well as an effect of 'good

---

[21]Desmond Anderson, "Achieving Community Consensus," *Public Management,* 48 (March 1966), 63.

government,' and that most of the cities that have it are, by these criteria, better governed than they otherwise would have been."[22] No important evidence is available that would contradict such an evaluation.[23]

Controversy centers on the manager not as administrator but as community leader. While most urban practitioners and writers agree that a city manager should exercise community leadership, some suggest that he cannot do so effectively no matter how hard he tries—especially if he attempts to be a major agent of change. We have pointed to resources a manager can use to influence community decisions, but the larger question of his overall political strengths and weaknesses remains unanswered.

Richard Neustadt has argued that even the policy strengths of the President depend not on his formal powers but rather on his power to persuade—"personal capacity to influence the conduct of men who make up the government."[24] The power to persuade is explained as the power to bargain (though Neustadt does note that the extraordinary status and authority of the President yield important bargaining advantages). In contrast to the President, the city manager persuades in far less favorable circumstances. By statute and custom, the manager is typed as a neutral administrator, not a community leader. While reputation and prestige can enhance his political status, the manager cannot, without explicit council endorsement, speak out to challenge public opinion on controversial policy issues. The lack of formal powers, the need for continuous legislative approval, and the public stereotype of an apolitical administrator place real constraints on the manager's power to persuade. The manager's primary resources become those of regulating or manipulating

---

22Banfield and Wilson, *City Politics,* p. 185.

23Quite the reverse—two political scientists found, for example, in a random sample study of 200 of the 309 American cities with populations of 50,000 or more, "Our data suggest that in 1960 when a city adopts reformed structures, it comes to be governed less on the basis of conflict and more on the basis of the rationalistic theory of administration." Robert Lineberry and Edmund Fowler, "Reformism and Public Policies in American Cities," *American Political Science Review,* 61 (September 1967), 710.

24Richard Neustadt, *Presidential Power* (New York: Mentor Books, 1964), p. 16; see also pp. 15–21, 42–63.

information and not direct and open persuasion for preferred policy outcomes.

The power to persuade also can be divided into participant and symbolic influences. The city manager has some major resources to bargain with community influentials or even his own council. Expertise, near monopoly of information, extensive contacts, and so forth allow the manager to be an active and important policy participant. Though uneven, he can exercise some face-to-face influence on nonroutine decisions. Yet when dealing with community traditions, values, and prejudices, and when attempting to achieve a working community consensus, the city manager cannot provide much in the way of symbolic leadership. Murray Edelman writes, "Politics is for most of us a passing parade of abstract symbols."[25] In most instances, the city manager cannot challenge the old or introduce major new political symbols. Rather, he is hired to be a spokesman for the dominant political ethos and secular values of the community. Thus the symbolic influences of the manager have to be indirect; for only rarely can he openly challenge the "passing parade of abstract symbols" of main-street politics.

Yet a discussion of the city manager's weakness in policy making requires a corrective perspective. For many critics seem to delight in making a case for the city manager's inability "to deal boldly with a city's larger problems." And, to some, the city manager bears heavy responsibility for the failure to solve various urban social, economic, and political ills. Certainly the litany for structural reform—for example, strong mayor or partisan elections—is partially fueled by these criticisms. What is ignored is the socioeconomic environment in which local decisions are made. The real question is whether any local executive, appointed or elected, can solve the problems that are responsible for the urban crisis. Probably the most powerful urban executive in America, Mayor Richard Daley of Chicago, faces repeated obstacles to nonroutine community decisions. In fact, Banfield in *Political Influence* devotes considerable space to the

---

[25]Murray Edelman, *The Symbolic Uses of Politics* (Urbana: University of Illinois Press, 1964), p. 5.

severe limitations on political innovation and leadership that are faced by Mayor Daley.[26] The point to stress is that the policy weaknesses of the manager are also in many ways the weaknesses of any local chief executive, be he manager, mayor, or commissioner.

City Manager as Community Leader

Power and Policy

Interpretations of the importance of the city manager as a community leader are replete with contradictions and what this writer believes to be ill-founded or superficial evaluations. To many local government textbook writers, the city manager represents the substance of the policy process—city politics is translated into the activities and duties of the manager and his councilmen. Municipal journals also seem to share this view; for they see the manager as a one-man show, initiating and presiding over the making of community decisions. By way of contrast, many scholars in search of community power almost ignore the city manager; at most, studies of who governs give the city manager a very modest role in community decision making. For example, in *Who's Running This Town*, Ritchie Lowry does not discuss either the position of city manager or its incumbents —even though the town, Chico, California, has had a city manager for many years. Still others see the city manager as a passive front man for business and commercial interests, as a prototype of an antidemocratic elitist, and even as responsible for a supposed growing trend toward democratic collectivism.[27]

Students of community power usually discover that many people take part in the community decision process and that leadership patterns vary. To say that the city manager governs is an

---

[26]Edward Banfield, *Political Influence* (New York: The Free Press, 1961), pp. 235–85.

[27]For an especially critical and wide-ranging indictment of the city manager, see Lincoln Smith, "The Manager System and Collectivism," *American Journal of Economics and Sociology*, 24 (January 1965), 21–38.

overstatement. Besides cultural and structural constraints, specialization and decentralization are pervasive. Though the scale is exaggerated for Bay Area cities, Banfield's description of Chicago makes the obvious but often unrecognized point of the chaos, diversity, and confusion of the local power structure:

> The Chicago area from a purely formal standpoint can hardly be said to have a government at all. There are hundreds, perhaps thousands, of bodies, each of which has a measure of legal authority and none of which has enough of it to carry out a course of action which other bodies oppose. . . . virtually nothing can be done if anyone opposes—and, of course, everything is always opposed by someone—and therefore every opponent's terms must always be met if there is to be action. Every outcome must therefore be an elaborate compromise if not stalemate.[28]

Beyond comments on the political setting and process, no existing study of a council-manager city has found the city manager to be the modern-day equivalent of a city boss. Rather, even the most influential and respected city managers rank only among other men at the top.

On the other hand, community decisions are made, *and* the city manager is one of the few who frequently participate, whether from interest or obligation, in community-wide decisions. The city manager, a colleague suggested, is probably the one local actor in a position to take a comprehensive view of the public interest and to exercise an important influence on other policy participants. The city manager also exercises policy leadership by default. For elected officials and civic or economic notables are usually unwilling to adopt a public position on an issue until widespread support or negligible opposition exists.[29] Someone has to fill the leadership vacuum and that someone is often the city manager. Many managers recognize and accept the demands to be community leaders; for example, one city manager responded as follows: "The city manager puts the time where the chief problems are. And this differs greatly with the circum-

---

[28]Banfield, *Political Influence*, p. 235.
[29]See C. N. Stone, "Leadership by Default," *National Civic Review*, 53 (July 1964), 360–64.

stances. Also, it depends on how much the council wants or will let the city manager assume leadership."

Though case studies have demonstrated that city managers engage in behavior resulting in determinative roles in community decision making, the manager's influence on community decisions should not be exaggerated. Even if superbly trained, highly skilled, blessed with a powerful personality and enormous political talents, the city manager is only one force in the community. The manager will face critical limits on what he can do. For example, *resources are scarce*—"Financing is a major problem. I just can't do the kind of job of building up that I would like to simply because we do not have much money. This means that I am unable to promote any large scale improvements"; *community consensus for change is difficult to achieve*—"It takes a long time to formulate an idea and then sell it to the council and the community. We have a good deal of opposition for opposition's sake in the community. There is at the same time a lack of community response to many new programs"; *formal authority is restricted*—"I have master plans coming out of my ears. It is frustrating to see what could be done and what we are doing. This does not sound very democratic, but when I see a problem where the solution is obvious, I think something ought to be done. Instead, long, arduous preparation is necessary to even make an attempt"; and *political support from councilmen is weak*—"The council really shirks its responsibilities; it does not decide issues based on the available information or on community needs. And upon making decisions, the council rarely sells its decisions to the public. Instead, political expediency marks decisions." Frustration rather than success characterizes most ventures of the city manager as community leader. For influences that counter manager leadership are many and important; the city manager is for most purposes resolutely constrained by situational, structural, cultural, and environmental factors.[30]

If the obstacles to manager leadership are many and impor-

[30]See Robert Alford, "The Comparative Study of Urban Politics," in *Urban Research and Policy Planning*, Leo Schnore and Henry Fagin, eds. (Beverly Hills, Calif.: Sage Publications, 1967), pp. 263–304.

tant, what real influence does a city manager have? It depends, of course; it depends on the city, council, partisans, issue, circumstances, and the city manager. The more fundamental question is whether the city manager makes any significant difference. Oliver Williams and colleagues in *Suburban Differences and Metropolitan Policies* find that municipal policies measured by expenditures are closely related to socioeconomic variables, that in other words most expenditure decisions could be explained by the socioeconomic environment using such factors as needs, preferences, and resources.[31] Moreover, major changes can result from new demands; yet while the manager may participate in meeting such demands, he will be working for more or less predictable solutions.

Nevertheless, the influence of the city manager cannot be dismissed. Decisions, writes William Gamson, "may singly or in aggregate have far reaching effects on the social structure and thus may change the kinds of limits that will operate on future decisions. And even small differences in choice can have very large consequences."[32] A manager, for example, could influence a decision on land use that could lead to the emergence of a major city policy, which could in turn shape the fate and character of the community. In much the same way, the decision of the manager not to exercise such influence could have similar consequences. For, as Theodore Sorensen reminds us, "each new decision sets a precedent, begetting new decisions, foreclosing others, and causing reactions which require counteraction."[33]

---

[31] A somewhat different emphasis can be found in a study by Eyestone and Eulau; they conclude, "policy is the result of the forcing effects of population size and growth, as mediated by the city group life, and the goals sought by policy makers, as expressed in their commitment to development and their attitude toward the scope of government activity. In some cases resource capability may be an important constraint on policy development, but the willingness of policy makers to tap available resources seems to be a more important variable in explaining the course of policy development." See Robert Eyestone and Heinz Eulau, "City Councils and Policy Outcomes: Developmental Profiles," in *City Politics and Public Policy*, James Q. Wilson, ed. (New York: John Wiley & Sons, 1968), p. 65.

[32] William Gamson, *Power and Discontent* (Homewood, Ill.: The Dorsey Press, 1968), p. 188.

[33] Theodore Sorensen, *Decision-Making in the White House* (New York: Columbia University Press, 1963), p. 20.

This writer has no inside information to describe, explain, or evaluate who gets what, when, and how in Bay Area cities. Yet while speculative, two influences of city managers probably have had a general impact. For one, city managers have placed great stress on professional management and its watchwords: efficiency, impartiality, and honesty. They have drawn upon the most recent administrative developments and applied them to the cities. More than one observer has concluded that Bay Area cities are remarkably well run and stand as superior in operation to their counterparts in county and state government. The second overall influence is the emphasis of managers on planning and general welfare in the community. While failures are as conspicuous as successes, city managers have emerged as guardians of the public interest and surely have contributed to the acceptance of the values of planning and its companion, progress.[34]

Responsible Democrat?

The widely heralded emergence of the city manager as a community leader has fostered another controversy: does the role of the city manager clash with democratic values? Supporters bestow praise on the manager as a responsible democrat; and, conversely, critics condemn the manager as an unresponsive technocrat. Such discussions are frequently confused and rendered unsatisfactory by disagreements, intended or not, on the definitions of words like *responsible* and *democrat*. And, in addition, most observers fail to distinguish myths and symbols from performance. The result—many critiques praise or debunk straw men, substituting good government rhetoric or ideological prejudices for precise criteria and empirical evidence. The question of what difference a city manager makes for democratic politics should be answered in the context of what actually happens.

While who governs depends on a variety of circumstances and values, almost every city is governed by some kind of an elite; for the decision structure is inevitably concentrated.[35] Even in the

---

[34]For example, see the appraisal of Charles Adrian and Charles Press, *Governing Urban America* (New York: McGraw-Hill, 1968), pp. 210–11.
[35]See Terry Clark, *Community Structure and Decision Making* (San Francisco: Chandler Publishing Company, 1968), especially pp. 91–128, 139–58.

New England town meetings, some people enjoy a disproportion-
ate amount of influence in what decisions are made. The crucial
matter, says Robert Presthus, "is the openness of the elite, the
ends to which its powers are devoted, the means used to achieve
them, and the methods available to the mass for changing and
controlling it."[36] As a member of the elite, what effect does the
city manager have on the democratic process? To evaluate the
democratic contribution of the city manager, let us examine the
manager in terms of the four criteria suggested by Presthus.

The obvious point to preface this discussion is that the city
manager is only one member of the political elite. And because
he is an outsider, a professional, and what Robert Merton calls
a cosmopolitan, the manager should not be viewed as a councilman might be viewed.[37] The evaluation is rather one of the manager as a democratic actor and the major consequences of his
participation in the community decision process.

1) "Openness of the elite"—Probably no member of the local
elite is more open to diverse public influences than the city
manager. As a legitimate public officeholder, he is by law a public
servant; the office if not the manager is highly visible to the
general public; and he—or members of his staff—are likely to
participate in more decisions than any other members of the
elite. Access to the manager is further fostered because he is
vulnerable to public wrath; citizens can be ignored only at high
risk to the manager's tenure. More often than not, the manager
spends much of his time in meetings with interested citizens,
community groups, and the public-at-large. His public and professional reputation depend to no small extent on the ability to
develop and sustain large amounts of goodwill. An open door
policy and numerous contacts expose the manager to a wide
range of demands. Moreover, the manager becomes an important
wedge in the power structure because he brings impartial in-

---

[36]Robert Presthus, *Men at the Top* (New York: Oxford University Press, 1964),
p. 11.
[37]City politics will continue, at least for the immediate future, to be dominated
by those whom Robert Merton has called locals. See Robert Merton, "Patterns
of Influence: Locals and Cosmopolitans," in *Social Theory and Social Structure*
(rev. ed.; Glencoe, Ill.: The Free Press, 1957), pp. 387–420.

formation and expertise to complex community decisions, requiring such decisions to be more than face-to-face bargaining
sessions among local notables. Finally, the manager often represents those whose interests are not represented in the elite.
Negroes provide a good example. The city manager tends to
go out of his way to resolve racial tensions and potential problems. Admittedly, reasons of peace and harmony loom as important as good intentions, but, regardless, the manager does
self-consciously represent sections of the public left outside of the
decision structure.

2) "End of the elite"—As a whole, managers view themselves
as political moderates in the abstract and pragmatic problem
solvers in practice; they articulate goals for the community that
are similar to what we called the Conservationist ideology; and,
perhaps most important, they share a public service orientation
and a commitment to the public good. The thrust of their policy
efforts is to make the community a better place to live and/or work.
Unlike, therefore, most elite members, the city manager champions the general welfare of the community as opposed, for example, to the special interests of business, labor, or civic groups.
That these values approximate what some observers call the
middle-class ideal should not be judged as antidemocratic but
as a part of a larger development:

> Perhaps in the next twenty or thirty years municipal affairs will
> pass entirely into the hands of honest, impartial, and nonpolitical
> "experts"; at any rate, this seems to be the logical fulfillment of
> the middle-class ideal.[38]

And if one accepts the optimistic predictions for the year 2000,
the middle-class ideal will be increasingly shared, for reasons of
higher education, income, and media penetration, by most people in American society.[39]

3) "Means of elite"—The political resources of the manager
are primarily those of office, time, information, expertise, and

---

[38]Edward Banfield, "The Political Implications of Metropolitan Growth," in
The Future Metropolis, Lloyd Dodwin, ed. (New York: Braziller, 1961), p. 96.
[39]See, for example, Herman Kahn and Anthony Wiener, *The Year 2000* (New
York: The Macmillan Company, 1967).

personal skills and reputation. Influence takes the form of gentle persuasion. The potential political resources of the manager are considerable, but so are the limits on his exercise of influence. Real or anticipated approval of the council and most members of the elite are necessary before a manager can forcefully push for his policy approach to a community issue or problem. While various specific and subtle strategies are open to the manager, law, custom, and elected officials require the manager to bargain for and build his policy case as a more or less faceless professional administrator. The result is that the manager exercises private influence by such informal methods as consultation, policy discussions, advising, and informal bringing together of information and data. The policy means of the manager would thus seem to contribute to and not detract from the democratic process by which people and their agents inform themselves, discuss, make compromises, and finally arrive at a decision.

A procedural criticism often made by political scientists is, that the city manager substitutes the administrative process for the political process in making policy decisions. The administrative process, translated as scientific government by apolitical experts, is seen as undemocratic in method—beyond popular control and participation. On nonroutine decisions, the charge is probably overstated if not ill-founded; for controversial issues, whether administrative or community-wide, cannot be resolved within city hall by the manager and his staff. But, even if true for some decisions, the administrative process should not be viewed as a mechanical decision structure run by and for technical experts. Rather, it is an institutional device through which a community realizes many of its values. As Peter Woll contends in *American Bureaucracy,* the administrative process may be more humane and democratic than the political process.[40] Reasons at the local level are several. In Bay Area cities, the manager's ideology of public interest, the effort to develop clientele and popular support, the multiple access of interested groups and citizens, the pass and review stages of administrative organization,

---

[40]See Peter Woll, *American Bureaucracy* (New York: W. W. Norton, 1963), especially pp. 174–77.

the concern for anticipated reactions, as well as the potential and actual supervision by the council make the administrative process far more democratic than the critics give it credit for. To survive, the city manager cannot make policy by scientific formulation but must pay attention to political demands from many sources in the community.

4) "Changing and controlling the elite"—No member of the elite is as open to change and control as the city manager. Rather than occupying an impregnable power redoubt, the city manager is one of the most dispensable men in any political community. Tenure among Bay Area managers is approximately five years. The close and jealous supervision of the city council requires that the city manager be highly responsive to their preferences and interests. If a city manager becomes too prominent, he can become an election target. Or if he pushes hard on a pet project, he becomes vulnerable to political retribution from those who objected. Groups that feel intensely about an issue can also bring strong influences to bear on the manager. Finally, the need for agreement on a controversial issue requires that the manager solicit support from others; this need for support means the manager is subject to extensive controls on his policy discretion.

City managers find themselves, regardless of personal choice, responsive and accountable to major community demands, interests, and values. The character and style of the manager's involvement in the policy process do not conflict with the possibilities and substance of representative democracy in urban communities. However, a major weakness in terms of democratic politics should be noticed. The city manager can primarily exercise only what we previously described as tentative, quiet leadership on controversial issues. He is unable to act as a political executive "to formulate and define purpose" because of important constraints. These constraints merit brief comment. First, the city council objects to the city manager as an independent political leader. Second, the manager's need for near unanimity on controversial nonroutine decisions in effect prohibits the manager from pushing hard on many community issues, actual and potential. And, third, the manager cannot exercise the symbolic leadership of a chief executive. And without command of dramatic political symbols, the manager cannot challenge old values, spotlight uncomfortable problems, or marshal strong public support. These arguments lead to the conclusion that although a responsible democrat, the city manager is often a weak political executive.

Prospect for the Future

What about the future? This study tells us about the attitudes and behavior characteristics of Bay Area managers in the middle 1960s. Predictions of the future are, however, deceptively difficult, speculative, and often wrong. Joseph Krutch, in a review essay on several studies of the future, made this common lament: "having listened to the confident voices of at least a score of intelligent and informed men, I am no more sure than I was before what the future has in store for us. There are so many conflicting forces making so many possibilities that there are a dozen possible futures, no one of which seems certain enough to justify saying, 'This is what it is going to be like.' "[41] The discussion of probable trends here will be short-range and not in the tradition of the Commission on the Year 2000. The city manager will be the focus, not the urban process or the future metropolis. The changes may be applauded or condemned, but, regardless, they would appear to be emerging parts of the council-manager practice in the Bay Area—and probably throughout the United States.

City managers occupy a position in transition; from being expert housekeepers, managers now have emerged as would-be community leaders. This change in emphasis if not function will have notable consequences for personal characteristics, policy orientation, and policy performance of city managers. New managers of the 1970s will increasingly share the same predispositions and prior experiences. College education will be all but mandatory. The typical manager will major as an undergraduate in one of the social sciences—probably political science, self-consciously decide to enter city management, and pursue graduate

---

[41]Joseph Krutch, "What the Year 2000 Won't Be Like," *Saturday Review,* 51 (January 20, 1968), 12.

work in political science or public administration. Appointments will be rare for those without previous experience in city management. The crises of our cities should recruit young men interested in social and political change; and the image of the manager as an agent of change and as a community leader should recruit those with distinct social and political skills. The new manager, in essence, will be recruited, trained, and prepared to assume community leadership.

The prospects for change in the policy orientation of city managers appear obvious. An executive orientation with a commitment to innovation and leadership should become the predominant policy perspective. Changes in recruitment, training, and circumstances permit no other conclusion. Managers should increasingly see themselves as political executives whose job includes advocating policy and securing council and community approval. The limits on what policy issues are proper for the manager to involve himself in should also expand. The manager will likely see himself as a leader in the areas of social progress and conflict, community identity, and future planning. So, if this study could be repeated in ten years, most of the Bay Area managers would express viewpoints that would now be classified as those orientations of a Political Leader or Political Executive.

Changes in orientation, events, and circumstances will mean that the city manager, especially in cities with over twenty thousand in population, will act more as a political executive than as an expert technician. Routine responsibility for efficient, effective, and economical administration will be delegated to the city staff. The manager will devote most of his personal time to policy and value questions and to community politics, bargaining and symbol making. Possibilities and demands for innovation and leadership will grow. Federal and, to a lesser extent, state government will encourage and fund programs that expand present, or lead the city into new, policy activities. Besides, traditional channels, communication in the forms of newsletters, surveys, mobile town halls, radio or even television time will be used to talk with and to involve city residents. The city planner should become an accepted spokesman for the good life as well as for greater control over the urban environment. Finally, the urban crisis should stimulate interest, evoke demands, and make available resources heretofore unanticipated. Thus, in the immediate future, the city manager is likely to become a major and influential activist in community decisions, concerned with the promotion and protection of social and human values.

The changes we have discussed have not resulted from reform of the council-manager plan. The original model authored by the progressive reform movement has remained more or less intact. Yet some formal changes are now taking place in order to facilitate, even to encourage, policy innovation and leadership. Three in the Bay Area, two minor and one major, merit comment. First —the manager, except in very small cities, no longer runs a one-man show. Instead, the city manager has an office of secretaries and assistants. Staff help provides the city manager with the time and advice to be a community leader. The trend toward increased staffing of the city manager's office will continue; and, further, it will provide an important channel of recruitment for bright, ambitious young men. Second—to reduce the job insecurity of the city manager, the practice of severance pay has been adopted in several Bay Area cities and meets with the strong endorsement of almost every city manager. Proponents argue that severance pay will encourage the city manager to push his policy views more strongly because he will have a paid period of time to look for another job if fired. Finally, the most important structural reform is the call for an elected mayor. While not a dramatic reform, it is a further indication of the manager's working for more policy leverage in dealing with community problems.

An elected mayor is a proposal of long standing. Moreover, it is not a radical reform—almost 50 percent of the council-manager cities in the United States now have elected mayors. But, in the Bay Area, city managers and other guardians of good government formerly rejected the need for an elected mayor. Now managers, especially in cities of over twenty thousand in population, stress the need for an elected mayor to assume the symbolic leadership of the city. Managers hope to get the city in a position where support and resources can be mobilized to attack many of the problems that only visionaries talk about. The number of

Bay Area cities with elected mayors is increasing and should continue to do so.[42]

The city manager, in conclusion, will continue as an able administrator and improve his position as a political executive in Bay Area cities. He will thrive as a respected professional and urban generalist, a necessary link between amateur politicians and expert administrators. However, the most important recommendation this study invites is that city councils need to redefine the policy role of the manager. City councils should see the manager as a policy partner and not as a rival or servant. For the quality of city life will increasingly depend on the manager's ability to bring his expertise and information to bear on the process and content of public policy.

---

[42]There is no question that a popularly elected mayor is not a policy role panacea for the city manager; instead, the results may be the reverse. For the city manager and the elected mayor are likely to clash over innovation and leadership prerogatives. The elected mayor often regards the city manager as his administrative assistant rather than a policy executive or community leader. In a study of council-manager cities in Florida, Gladys Kammerer concludes, "A role collision of significant proportions may be said to exist in council-manager cities with popularly elected mayors . . . if the political end sought in a particular community is to enhance popular control and reduce authority of an appointed administrator, or at least to frustrate that appointed administrator, then the structural arrangement to accomplish this in council-manager government is to elect the mayor by popular vote." Gladys Kammerer, "Role Diversity of City Managers," *Administrative Science Quarterly,* 8 (March 1964), 440–442. There is now in the Bay Area considerable evidence to support this proposition. Thus, the city manager will likely find himself again disappointed if not doubly frustrated in his efforts to commit the resources of city government to his definition of the public interest or to achieve professional objectives for urban change. Yet given their lack of symbolic powers, most managers of large cities see no alternative except an elected mayor. (To a 1968 ICMA Goals Questionnaire administered by the League of California Cities, almost 70 percent of the managers who responded said they favored a strong mayor who would exercise political leadership.)

Appendixes

Appendix A

City Manager Interview Schedule

City Manager Interview Schedule

Interview Number _____

Name _____

City _____

	First Visit	Second Visit	Third Visit
Date			
Time			
Place			

Impressions

Frankness   Very Frank ( )
Frank ( )
Not Very Frank ( )
Very Evasive ( )

Cooperativeness   Very Cooperative ( )
Cooperative ( )
Not Very Cooperative ( )
Very Uncooperative ( )

Personal Characteristics

City Manager Questionnaire

1. To begin, how long have you been here in _____?

2. What do you think of _____ as a community in which to be a city manager?

   Probe: How is support for the council-manager plan?

3. I have a further question about _____. Communities are incorporated for different reasons, perform different functions. Here is a list of four kinds of city government. Would you rank the four in the order which they most closely describe _____.

   _____ 1. Our city government promotes community growth. We facilitate and encourage commercial and industrial expansion.

   _____ 2. Our city government promotes "suburban" living. We provide a high level of community services.

   _____ 3. Our city government promotes small government, low taxation. We limit community growth, maintain traditional services.

   _____ 4. Our city government is unable to promote any one interest. We work out policies with a number of conflicting community interests.

   Comments:

4. As you well know, there are always problems in every community. In your opinion, what two problems are most pressing in _____?

5. All right, you noted _____ as a problem. Generally speaking, what have you or will you recommend to the council to meet the _____ problem?

6. OK. The second problem you noted was _____. Generally speaking, what have you or will you recommend to the council to meet the _____ problem?

7. Next, I would like to ask you several questions about your philosophy and activities as city manager. To begin, why did you go into city management?

8. A city manager's reputation is said to depend on the approval of a number of different publics. Some publics, however, are probably more important than others. How would you rank the following on the importance of their approval to your reputation as a city manager?

_____ Administrative Staff
_____ Fellow City Managers
_____ Public-At-Large
_____ Council
_____ Community Groups
_____ Professional Management Groups

Comments:

8a. In the counties of Alameda, Contra Costa, Marin, San Mateo, and Santa Clara, whom do you regard as the five most outstanding city managers?

_____ _____

_____ _____

_____

9. The ICMA literature talks about the city manager profession. Frankly, what does it mean to you to be a member of the city manager profession?
Probes: Do you take an active role in professional associations?
Do you attend conferences? Local? National?
What municipal periodicals do you regularly read?

10. As a city manager, what are the most important things you have or expect to accomplish?

11. Generally speaking, would you describe yourself as a liberal, moderate, or conservative?

Probe: What does this label mean to you?

11a. Here is a list of 12 questions probing your political-economic philosophy. Mark each statement at the box to the right according to how much you agree or disagree with it.

For each question, choose one of the six possible answers:

      plus 1—I agree a little
      plus 2—I agree pretty much
      plus 3—I agree very much
      minus 1—I disagree a little
      minus 2—I disagree pretty much
      minus 3—I disagree very much

1. When private enterprise does not do the job well, it is up to the government to step in and meet the public's need for housing, water, power, and the like. _____

2. Men like Henry Ford and J. P Morgan, who overcame all competition on the road to success, are models for all young people to admire and imitate. _____

3. The government should own and operate all public utilities (gas, electric, water). _____

4. In general, full economic security is bad. Most men would not work if they did not need the money for eating and living. _____

5. The only way to do away with poverty is to make basic changes in our political and economic system._____

6. There should be some upper limit such as $50,000 per year on how much a person can earn. _____

7. At this time, powerful big business is a greater danger to our national welfare than powerful big unions. _____

8. We need more government controls over business practices and profits. _____

9. Labor unions in large corporations should be given a larger part in deciding company policy. _____

10. The government should develop a program of health insurance and medical care. _____

11. America may not be perfect, but the American way has brought us about as close as human beings can get to a perfect society. _____

12. Strong labor unions are necessary if the working man is to obtain greater security and a better standard of living. _____

12. I would like to ask you about your future plans as city manager of _____. Would you say that (1) I like this city and plan to stay on indefinitely; (2) I do not like this city and am looking for another city managership; (3) I plan to leave city management for some other type of work; or (4) I like this city, but I hope to move on to a larger city as a manager in the future.

    _____ 1.
    _____ 2.
    _____ 3.
    _____ 4.

13. Thank you very much. Now, ever since the council-manager plan was first adopted, there has been much disagreement over what a city manager should or should not do. How would you describe the job of a city manager—what are the most important things you should or should not do as a city manager?

    (IF RELEVANT) *Probe:* How about on matters of policy?

14. What would you say are the two most pressing problems or frustrations you face as city manager?

15. Here are ten questions on the job of being a city manager. Read each question and then decide which one of the four answers most closely describes how you feel—do you strongly agree, tend to agree, strongly disagree, or tend to disagree?

    Directions:
    1. Read each question carefully.
    2. Draw a line under the answer you select.

    1. A CITY MANAGER SHOULD ADVOCATE MAJOR CHANGES IN CITY POLICIES.
       A–strongly agree   B–tend to agree
       C–strongly disagree   D–tend to disagree

    2. A CITY MANAGER SHOULD GIVE A HELPING HAND TO GOOD COUNCILMEN WHO ARE COMING UP FOR REELECTION.
       A–strongly agree   B–tend to agree
       C–strongly disagree   D–tend to disagree

3.   A CITY MANAGER SHOULD MAINTAIN A NEUTRAL STAND ON
     ANY ISSUES ON WHICH THE COMMUNITY IS DIVIDED.
     A–strongly agree   B–tend to agree
     C–strongly disagree   D–tend to disagree

4.   A CITY MANAGER SHOULD CONSULT WITH THE COUNCIL
     BEFORE DRAFTING HIS OWN BUDGET PROPOSAL.
     A–strongly agree   B–tend to agree
     C–strongly disagree   D–tend to disagree

5.   A CITY MANAGER SHOULD OFFER THE COUNCIL AN OPINION
     ONLY WHEN HIS OPINION IS REQUESTED.
     A–strongly agree   B–tend to agree
     C–strongly disagree   D–tend to disagree

6.   A CITY MANAGER SHOULD ASSUME LEADERSHIP IN SHAPING
     MUNICIPAL POLICIES.
     A–strongly agree   B–tend to agree
     C–strongly disagree   D–tend to disagree

7.   A CITY MANAGER SHOULD ENCOURAGE PEOPLE WHOM HE
     RESPECTS TO RUN FOR THE CITY COUNCIL.
     A–strongly agree   B–tend to agree
     C–strongly disagree   D–tend to disagree

8.   A CITY MANAGER SHOULD ACT AS AN ADMINISTRATOR AND
     LEAVE POLICY MATTERS TO THE COUNCIL.
     A–strongly agree   B–tend to agree
     C–strongly disagree   D–tend to disagree

9.   A CITY MANAGER SHOULD ADVOCATE POLICIES TO WHICH
     IMPORTANT PARTS OF THE COMMUNITY MAY BE HOSTILE.
     A–strongly agree   B–tend to agree
     C–strongly disagree   D–tend to disagree

10. A CITY MANAGER SHOULD WORK THROUGH THE MOST POW-
     ERFUL MEMBERS OF THE COMMUNITY TO ACHIEVE POLICY
     GOALS.
     A–strongly agree   B–tend to agree
     C–strongly disagree   D–tend to disagree

16. Next, here are the same questions with one very important change. Rather than how you feel, answer in terms of what you do here in _____ —do you always, often, occasionally, seldom, or never?

   1. I ADVOCATE MAJOR CHANGES IN CITY POLICIES.
      A–always   B–often   C–occasionally
      D–seldom   E–never

   2. I GIVE A HELPING HAND TO GOOD COUNCILMEN WHO ARE COMING UP FOR REELECTION.
      A–always   B–often   C–occasionally
      D–seldom   E–never

   3. I MAINTAIN A NEUTRAL STAND ON ANY ISSUES ON WHICH THE COMMUNITY IS DIVIDED.
      A–always   B–often   C–occasionally
      D–seldom   E–never

   4. I CONSULT WITH THE COUNCIL BEFORE DRAFTING MY OWN BUDGET PROPOSAL.
      A–always   B–often   C–occasionally
      D–seldom   E–never

   5. I ASSUME LEADERSHIP IN SHAPING MUNICIPAL POLICIES.
      A–always   B–often   C–occasionally
      D–seldom   E–never

   6. I ENCOURAGE PEOPLE WHOM I RESPECT TO RUN FOR THE CITY COUNCIL.
      A–always   B–often   C–occasionally
      D–seldom   E–never

   7. I OFFER THE COUNCIL AN OPINION ONLY WHEN MY OPINION IS REQUESTED.
      A–always   B–often   C–occasionally
      D–seldom   E–never

   8. I ACT AS AN ADMINISTRATOR AND LEAVE POLICY MATTERS TO THE COUNCIL.
      A–always   B–often   C–occasionally
      D–seldom   E–never

9. I ADVOCATE POLICIES TO WHICH IMPORTANT PARTS OF THE
   COMMUNITY MAY BE HOSTILE.
   A–always   B–often   C–occasionally
   D–seldom   E–never

10. I WORK THROUGH THE MOST POWERFUL MEMBERS OF THE
    COMMUNITY TO ACHIEVE POLICY GOALS.
    A–always   B–often   C–occasionally
    D–seldom   E–never

17. Now I would like to ask you about the job of councilman.
    How would you describe the job of being a councilman—
    that is, what are the most important things a councilman
    should do?

18. One writer in the field of local government says, "The role
    of the council has emerged as a reviewing and vetoing agency,
    checking upon the city manager more than leading him in
    terms of policy making." Do you agree or disagree with this
    statement?

19. Is there much council disagreement on policy proposals?
    What usually accounts for the divisions on the council?

20. The activities of city mayors vary widely from city to city.
    In _____, what does the mayor do?

    Probe: How about in regard to policy making?

21. Next, let's talk about groups and organizations in _____.
    What are the most influential groups or organizations in city
    politics?

21a. How do you feel about the efforts of groups to make their
     views known to you and to seek your support?

22. Before making policy recommendations, do you ever seek
    support from any community groups? May I ask from which
    groups you have sought support?

23. One last question on groups in_____. Overall, would you describe the politics of_____as (1) very stable, with very few controversial questions that divide the community; (2) stable, despite a few controversial questions that divide the community; (3) subject to marked changes in groups controlling city government from one election to another as a result of policy controversies; or (4) subject to change of control from one election to another based upon personalities of candidates, not issues.

    _____ 1.
    _____ 2.
    _____ 3.
    _____ 4.

    Comments:

24. Now, I would like to ask you some general questions about your relationship with members of the city council. About what proportion of your time per week is spent in conferring with councilmen?

25. In a research report, I read this quote by a city manager, "One of the most delicate tasks of the city manager is to educate his council without their knowledge." How do you feel about this?

26. Now, as far as your participation in policy making is concerned, what does the council expect you to do or not to do?

27. An ICMA pamphlet says there are policy areas where city managers push hard and other policy areas where they remain neutral or stay out. In what policy areas do you push hard? Remain neutral or stay out?

28. Returning now to your relationship with council members, here is a list of statements which describe the behavior of individuals in leadership positions. There are five possible answers to each question: always, often, occasionally, seldom,

or never. Decide which one of the five most closely describes your behavior as city manager.

1. I EXPLAIN WHY A PARTICULAR POLICY IS IMPORTANT.
   A–always   B–often   C–occasionally
   D–seldom   E–never

2. I MAKE CONTACTS OUTSIDE OF CITY HALL FOR THE COUNCIL.
   A–always   B–often   C–occasionally
   D–seldom   E–never

3. I SCHEDULE THE POLICIES TO BE TAKEN UP.
   A–always   B–often   C–occasionally
   D–seldom   E–never

4. I STRESS THE IMPORTANCE OF COOPERATION AMONG COUNCIL MEMBERS.
   A–always   B–often   C–occasionally
   D–seldom   E–never

5. I DO PERSONAL FAVORS FOR COUNCIL MEMBERS.
   A–always   B–often   C–occasionally
   D–seldom   E–never

6. I GIVE THE COUNCIL ADVANCE NOTICE OF POLICY CHANGES.
   A–always   B–often   C–occasionally
   D–seldom   E–never

7. I STAND UP FOR COUNCIL POLICY EVEN IF IT IS UNPOPULAR.
   A–always   B–often   C–occasionally
   D–seldom   E–never

8. I ENCOURAGE THE COUNCIL MEMBERS TO WORK AS A TEAM.
   A–always   B–often   C–occasionally
   D–seldom   E–never

9. I FOLLOW STATE AND CHARTER PROCEDURES TO THE LETTER.
   A–always   B–often   C–occasionally
   D–seldom   E–never

10. I INVITE COUNCIL MEMBERS TO MY HOME.
    A–always   B–often   C–occasionally
    D–seldom   E–never

11. I KEEP THE COUNCIL WELL INFORMED ON POLICY MATTERS.
    A–always   B–often   C–occasionally
    D–seldom   E–never

12. I SPEAK IN PUBLIC IN THE NAME OF THE COUNCIL.
    A–always   B–often   C–occasionally
    D–seldom   E–never

13. I PLAN AHEAD ON WHAT SHOULD BE DONE.
    A–always   B–often   C–occasionally
    D–seldom   E–never

14. I SIDE WITH THE SAME COUNCIL MEMBERS IN CASE OF DIS-
    AGREEMENT.
    A–always   B–often   C–occasionally
    D–seldom   E–never

15. I SUGGEST NEW APPROACHES TO PROBLEMS.
    A–always   B–often   C–occasionally
    D–seldom   E–never

16. I CALL COUNCILMEN BY THEIR FIRST NAMES.
    A–always   B–often   C–occasionally
    D–seldom   E–never

17. I KEEP INFORMED ON HOW COUNCILMEN THINK AND FEEL
    ABOUT POLICY MATTERS.
    A–always   B–often   C–occasionally
    D–seldom   E–never

18. I BACK UP COUNCIL MEMBERS IN THEIR POLICY ACTIONS.
    A–always   B–often   C–occasionally
    D–seldom   E–never

19. I MEET INFORMALLY WITH COUNCIL MEMBERS AT REGU-
    LARLY SCHEDULED TIMES.
    A–always   B–often   C–occasionally
    D–seldom   E–never

20. I HELP MEMBERS OF THE COUNCIL SETTLE THEIR CONFLICTS.
    A–always   B–often   C–occasionally
    D–seldom   E–never

21.   I ENCOURAGE COUNCIL MEMBERS TO PUSH NEW POLICIES.
      A–always   B–often   C–occasionally
      D–seldom   E–never

22.   I ATTEND SOCIAL EVENTS OF THE COUNCIL MEMBERS.
      A–always   B–often   C–occasionally
      D–seldom   E–never

23.   I WAIT FOR THE COUNCIL TO PUSH NEW POLICIES.
      A–always   B–often   C–occasionally
      D–seldom   E–never

24.   I ASK THAT COUNCIL MEMBERS FOLLOW CHARTER OR STATE
      REGULATIONS.
      A–always   B–often   C–occasionally
      D–seldom   E–never

25.   I ADVOCATE NEW POLICIES TO THE COUNCIL.

      A–always   B–often   C–occasionally
      D–seldom   E–never

29.   One question on a problem that concerns all cities. Some
      people feel that every city has problems which it cannot
      solve by itself, but which require some kind of area-wide
      solution. I am wondering how you feel about these metro-
      politan problems?

      Probe: How about solutions to these problems?

30.   Finally, I have a few more personal questions about yourself.
      In what year were you born?

31.   What local clubs or organizations—professional, fraternal, or
      service—do you belong to? Are you an officer? Are you active
      or not very active?

32.   Generally speaking, do you think of yourself as a Repub-
      lican, Democrat, or Independent?

33.   Where did you go to college? What was your major?

34. Did you go to graduate school? Where? What did you specialize in?

35. Since then, have you had any specialized training in city management?

36. Briefly, could you sketch your occupational career?

Appendix B

City Manager Questionnaire

Overall Instructions

Answer carefully all questions;
Make comments, if necessary;
Mark the most satisfactory answer.*

I thank you for your care and cooperation.

Dr. Ronald O. Loveridge

---

1. For a variety of reasons, some cities are viewed by fellow city managers as better than others. Overall, do you find _____ to be an excellent, good, average, or unsatisfactory city in which to be a city manager? Check one!

   _____ A. Excellent
   _____ B. Good
   _____ C. Average
   _____ D. Unsatisfactory
   _____ E. Don't know

   Comments: _____

   _____

---

*Some answers might seem inapplicable to your city; nevertheless, for the study's purposes, mark the most nearly appropriate answer.

2. Communities are incorporated for different reasons, perform different functions. Here is a list of four kinds of city government. Would you rank them from 1 to 4 in the order which they most closely describe _____.
    (We hope to get at the emphases of city governments.)

    _____ A.   Our city government promotes community growth. We facilitate and encourage commercial and industrial expansion.

    _____ B.   Our city government promotes "suburban" living. We provide a high level of community services.

    _____ C.   Our city government promotes small government, low taxation. We limit community growth, maintain traditional services.

    _____ D.   Our city government is unable to promote any one interest. We work out policies with a number of conflicting community interests.

    Comments: _____

    _____

3. In general, would you describe the politics of _____ as (A) very stable, with very few controversial questions that divide the community; (B) stable, despite some controversial questions that divide the community; or (C) unstable, subject to major controversies on important policy questions. Check one!

    _____ A.   Very Stable
    _____ B.   Stable
    _____ C.   Unstable

    Comments: _____

    _____

4. Moving from the community to your position as city manager, I have several questions. A city manager's reputation is said to depend on the approval of a number of different

publics. Some publics, however, are probably more important than others. How would you rank the following on their importance to your reputation as a city manager? Rank from 1 to 6: 1 means most important . . . 6 means least important.

_____ A. Administrative Staff
_____ B. Fellow City Managers
_____ C. Public-At-Large
_____ D. Council
_____ E. Community Groups
_____ F. Professional Management Groups

Comments: _____

_____

5. The ICMA literature talks about the city manager profession. Frankly, what does it mean to you to be a member of the city manager profession? Do you feel it is very important, somewhat important, not very important, or unimportant? Check one!

_____ A. Very Important
_____ B. Somewhat Important
_____ C. Not Very Important
_____ D. Unimportant

Comments: _____

_____

6. Do you attend all, most, some, few, or none of the city manager conferences sponsored by the League of California Cities? Check one!

_____ A. All
_____ B. Most
_____ C. Some
_____ D. Few
_____ E. None

Comments: _____

_____

7. In the nine counties making up the Bay Region (Alameda, Contra Costa, Marin, Napa, San Mateo, Solano, Sonoma, San Francisco, and Santa Clara), whom do you regard as the five most outstanding city managers? Please write in five names.

_____   _____

_____   _____

_____

8. One question about your future plans as city manager of _____. Would you say that (A) I like this city and plan to stay on indefinitely; (B) I do not like this city and am looking for another city managership; (C) I plan to leave city management for some other type of work; or (D) I like this city, but I hope to move on to another city as a manager in the future. Check one!

_____ A. I like this city and plan to stay on indefinitely;

_____ B. I do not like this city and am looking for another city managership;

_____ C. I plan to leave city management for some other type of work;

_____ D. I like this city, but I hope to move on to another city as a manager in the future.

Comments: _____

_____

9. Generally speaking, would you describe yourself as a political liberal, moderate, or conservative?

_____ A. Conservative

_____ B. Moderate

_____ C. Liberal

Comments: _____

_____

10. Again, generally speaking, do you think of yourself as a Republican, Democrat, or Independent?

_____ A. Strong Democrat
_____ B. Weak Democrat
_____ C. Independent
_____ D. Weak Republican
_____ E. Strong Republican

Comments: _____

_____

11. Here is a list of 12 questions about politics and economics. Mark each statement according to how much you agree or disagree with it. In other words, select the response which most closely describes how you feel. For each question, choose one of the six possible answers:

(+) plus 1—I agree a little
(+) plus 2—I agree pretty much
(+) plus 3—I agree very much
(—) minus 1—I disagree a little
(—) minus 2—I disagree pretty much
(—) minus 3—I disagree very much

_____ A. When private enterprise does not do the job well, it is up to the government to step in and meet the public's need for housing, water, power, and the like.

_____ B. Men like Henry Ford and J. P. Morgan, who overcame all competition on the road to success, are models for all young people to admire and imitate.

_____ C. The government should own and operate all public utilities (gas, electric, water).

_____ D. In general, full economic security is bad. Most men would not work if they did not need the money for eating and living.

_____ E. The only way to do away with poverty is to make basic changes in our political and economic system.

_____ F. There should be some upper limit such as $50,000 per year on how much a person can earn.

_____ G. At this time, powerful big business is a greater danger to our national welfare than powerful big unions.

_____ H. We need more government controls over business practices and profits.

_____ I. Labor unions in large corporations should be given a larger part in deciding company policy.

_____ J. The government should develop a program of health insurance and medical care.

_____ K. America may not be perfect, but the American way has brought us about as close as human beings can get to a perfect society.

_____ L. Strong labor unions are necessary if the working man is to obtain greater security and a better standard of living.

Comments: _____

_____

12. Thank you very much. Now ever since the council-manager plan was first adopted, there has been much disagreement over what a city manager should or should not do. Here are nine questions on the job of being a city manager. Read each question and then decide which one of the four answers most

closely describes how you feel—do you strongly agree, tend to agree, tend to disagree, or strongly disagree? Circle the answer you select!

1. A CITY MANAGER SHOULD ADVOCATE MAJOR CHANGES IN CITY POLICIES.
   A–strongly agree   B–tend to agree
   C–tend to disagree   D–strongly disagree

2. A CITY MANAGER SHOULD GIVE A HELPING HAND TO GOOD COUNCILMEN WHO ARE COMING UP FOR REELECTION.
   A–strongly agree   B–tend to agree
   C–tend to disagree   D–strongly disagree

3. A CITY MANAGER SHOULD MAINTAIN A NEUTRAL STAND ON ANY ISSUES ON WHICH THE COMMUNITY IS DIVIDED.
   A–strongly agree   B–tend to agree
   C–tend to disagree   D–strongly disagree

4. A CITY MANAGER SHOULD CONSULT WITH THE COUNCIL BE-FORE DRAFTING HIS OWN BUDGET.
   A–strongly agree   B–tend to agree
   C–tend to disagree   D–strongly disagree

5. A CITY MANAGER SHOULD ASSUME LEADERSHIP IN SHAPING MUNICIPAL POLICIES.
   A–strongly agree   B–tend to agree
   C–tend to disagree   D–strongly disagree

6. A CITY MANAGER SHOULD ENCOURAGE PEOPLE WHOM HE RESPECTS TO RUN FOR THE CITY COUNCIL.
   A–strongly agree   B–tend to agree
   C–tend to disagree   D–strongly disagree

7. A CITY MANAGER SHOULD ACT AS AN ADMINISTRATOR AND LEAVE POLICY MATTERS TO THE COUNCIL.
   A–strongly agree   B–tend to agree
   C–tend to disagree   D–strongly disagree

8. A CITY MANAGER SHOULD ADVOCATE POLICIES TO WHICH IMPORTANT PARTS OF THE COMMUNITY MAY BE HOSTILE.
   A–strongly agree   B–tend to agree
   C–tend to disagree   D–strongly disagree

9. A CITY MANAGER SHOULD WORK THROUGH THE MOST POWER-
   FUL MEMBERS OF THE COMMUNITY TO ACHIEVE POLICY
   GOALS.
   A–strongly agree   B–tend to agree
   C–tend to disagree   D–strongly disagree

Comments: _____

_____

13. Now, as far as your participation in policy making is con-
    cerned, the council probably has some pretty definite ex-
    pectations. Which of the following statements most closely
    describes what the council expects you to do? Check one!

    _____ A. Advise council (answer questions, give back-
                   ground information).
    _____ B. Participate in policy making process (in
                   some form, e.g., develop pros and cons, pro-
                   vide guidelines).
    _____ C. Develop and recommend policy, but primar-
                   ily in well defined policy areas.
    _____ D. Be a policy leader (initiate, recommend,
                   and take a position on most policy matters).

Comments: _____

_____

14. Moving from what is expected to what actually happens in
    _____, several questions are in order. One writer in the
    field of local government says, "The role of the council has
    emerged as a reviewing and vetoing agency, checking upon
    the city manager more than leading him in terms of policy
    making." Do you strongly agree, tend to agree, tend to dis-
    agree, or strongly disagree with this statement? Check one!

    _____ A. Strongly agree
    _____ B. Tend to agree
    _____ C. Tend to disagree
    _____ D. Strongly disagree

Comments: _____

_____

15. From the general to the more specific, how are the following things actually done in your city? Check one answer per problem!

    (1)   Hiring of department head:

            _____ A. Council chooses.

            _____ B. Council joins with manager in choosing.

            _____ C. Manager seeks council approval of his choice.

            _____ D. Manager chooses, but informs council before acting, so that if there are strong objections he can reconsider.

            _____ E. Manager hires then informs council.

            _____ F. Other

            _____ G. Not applicable

    (2)   Preparing the budget:

            _____ A. Council draws up the budget with or without the assistance of the manager.

            _____ B. Council instructs the manager regarding the main aspects of each departmental budget before he draws up the budget.

            _____ C. Manager gets general indication of whether council favors an "economy" or "expanded services" budget before he draws up the budget.

            _____ D. Manager prepares both an "economy" budget and an "expanded services" budget for the council's choice.

            _____ E. Manager prepares the budget without consulting council.

            _____ F. Other

            _____ G. Not applicable

(3) Requests for new or expanded services:

_____ A. Manager takes no part in initiating or commenting on proposals for new or expanded services.

_____ B. Council proposes and gets manager's opinion.

_____ C. Manager asks council whether it would consider expansion of services before he brings in proposals.

_____ D. Manager first suggests expansion of services only in informal or closed council sessions.

_____ E. Manager does not hesitate to propose expanded services which he feels are advisable.

_____ F. Other

_____ G. Not applicable

(4) Determination of company to which award of major purchasing contract will be made:

_____ A. Council takes bids and decides.

_____ B. Manager takes bids, forwards to council without recommendation, and council decides.

_____ C. Council takes bids, manager recommends, and council decides.

_____ D. Manager takes bids, makes recommendations, and council decides.

_____ E. Manager takes bids and decides.

_____ F. Other

_____ G. Not applicable

(5) Initiation of policy matters:

_____ A. Council initiates all policy matters.

_____ B. Council initiates most policy matters.

_____ C. Manager initiates most policy matters.

_____ D. Manager initiates all policy matters.

_____ E. Manager and council equally initiate policy matters.
_____ F. Other
_____ G. Not applicable

Comments: _____

_____

16. In a research report, I read this quote by a city manager, "One of the most delicate and important tasks of the city manager is to educate his council without their knowledge." Do you strongly agree, tend to agree, tend to disagree, or strongly disagree with this statement? Check one!

_____ A. Strongly agree
_____ B. Tend to agree
_____ C. Tend to disagree
_____ D. Strongly disagree

Comments: _____

_____

17. To focus again on the actual activities of city managers, here are eleven questions. Circle the answers which most accurately describe how you behave as city manager. (One circled answer per question!)

1. I ADVOCATE MAJOR CHANGES IN CITY POLICIES.
   A–always   B–often   C–occasionally
   D–seldom   E–never

2. I GIVE A HELPING HAND TO GOOD COUNCILMEN WHO ARE COMING UP FOR REELECTION.
   A–always   B–often   C–occasionally
   D–seldom   E–never

3. I MAINTAIN A NEUTRAL STAND ON ANY ISSUES ON WHICH THE COMMUNITY IS DIVIDED.
   A–always   B–often   C–occasionally
   D–seldom   E–never

4. I CONSULT WITH THE COUNCIL BEFORE DRAFTING MY OWN
   BUDGET PROPOSAL.
   A–always   B–often   C–occasionally
   D–seldom   E–never

5. I ASSUME LEADERSHIP IN SHAPING MUNICIPAL POLICIES.
   A–always   B–often   C–occasionally
   D–seldom   E–never

6. I ENCOURAGE PEOPLE WHOM I RESPECT TO RUN FOR THE
   CITY COUNCIL.
   A–always   B–often   C–occasionally
   D–seldom   E–never

7. I ACT AS AN ADMINISTRATOR AND LEAVE POLICY MATTERS
   TO THE COUNCIL.
   A–always   B–often   C–occasionally
   D–seldom   E–never

8. I ADVOCATE POLICIES TO WHICH IMPORTANT PARTS OF THE
   COMMUNITY MAY BE HOSTILE.
   A–always   B–often   C–occasionally
   D–seldom   E–never

9. I WORK THROUGH THE MOST POWERFUL MEMBERS OF THE
   COMMUNITY TO ACHIEVE POLICY GOALS.
   A–always   B–often   C–occasionally
   D–seldom   E–never

10. I WORK INFORMALLY WITH COUNCILMEN TO PREPARE IM-
    PORTANT POLICY PROPOSALS.
    A–always   B–often   C–occasionally
    D–seldom   E–never

11. I NOT ONLY PROVIDE POLICY INFORMATION BUT ALSO MAKE
    KNOWN MY OWN VIEWPOINT.
    A–always   B–often   C–occasionally
    D–seldom   E–never

Comments: _____

_____

18. Looking now at your relationship with council members, here is a list of eleven statements which describe the behavior of individuals in leadership positions. There are five possible answers to each question: always, often, occasionally, seldom, or never. Circle the answer which most closely describes your behavior as city manager.

  1. I SCHEDULE MOST OF THE POLICIES TAKEN UP BY THE COUNCIL.
      A–always   B–often   C–occasionally
      D–seldom   E–never

  2. I STRESS THE IMPORTANCE OF COOPERATION AMONG COUNCIL MEMBERS.
      A–always   B–often   C–occasionally
      D–seldom   E–never

  3. I DO PERSONAL FAVORS FOR COUNCIL MEMBERS.
      A–always   B–often   C–occasionally
      D–seldom   E–never

  4. I ENCOURAGE THE COUNCIL MEMBERS TO WORK AS A TEAM.
      A–always   B–often   C–occasionally
      D–seldom   E–never

  5. I INVITE COUNCIL MEMBERS TO MY HOME.
      A–always   B–often   C–occasionally
      D–seldom   E–never

  6. I SPEAK IN PUBLIC IN THE NAME OF THE COUNCIL.
      A–always   B–often   C–occasionally
      D–seldom   E–never

  7. I SIDE WITH THE SAME COUNCIL MEMBERS IN CASE OF DISAGREEMENT.
      A–always   B–often   C–occasionally
      D–seldom   E–never

  8. I MEET INFORMALLY WITH INDIVIDUAL COUNCIL MEMBERS.
      A–always   B–often   C–occasionally
      D–seldom   E–never

9. I ENCOURAGE COUNCIL MEMBERS TO PUSH NEW POLICIES.
   A–always   B–often   C–occasionally
   D–seldom   E–never

10. I ATTEND SOCIAL EVENTS OF THE COUNCIL MEMBERS.
    A–always   B–often   C–occasionally
    D–seldom   E–never

11. I ADVOCATE NEW POLICIES TO THE COUNCIL.
    A–always   B–often   C–occasionally
    D–seldom   E–never

Comments: _____

_____

19. Now, taking up some of the Bay Area's problems, would you indicate which level of government you feel should have the primary responsibility for handling and solving these problems. Please check one level per problem.

	City	Special District	County	ABAG	Bay Area District	State
Water Pollution						
Air Pollution						
Recreational Developments						
San Francisco Bay Fill						
Preserving Open Spaces						
Racial Discrimination						

20. Finally, I have a few personal questions about yourself. Your age group:

   _____ A.   under 30
   _____ B.   30–34
   _____ C.   35–39
   _____ D.   40–44

_____ E.   45–49
_____ F.   50–59
_____ G.   60 or above

21. Highest level of education which you have completed. Check
     one!

     _____ A.   High school
     _____ B.   1–2 years of college
     _____ C.   Over 2 years of college, but without degree
     _____ D.   Undergraduate degree
     _____ E.   Undergraduate degree and some graduate
                    work, but no degree
     _____ F.   Law degree
     _____ G.   Master's degree
     _____ H.   Other, please explain _____

22. Undergraduate degree field of specialization. Check one!

     _____ A.   Engineering
     _____ B.   Physical and natural sciences
     _____ C.   Architecture and planning
     _____ D.   Accounting
     _____ E.   Political Science or Government
     _____ F.   Economics, history, sociology
     _____ G.   Journalism, English
     _____ H.   Business administration
     _____ I.   Public administration
     _____ J.   Other: _____

23. Master's degree field of specialization. Check one!

     _____ A.   Engineering
     _____ B.   Physical and natural science
     _____ C.   Architecture and planning
     _____ D.   Accounting
     _____ E.   Political Science or Government
     _____ F.   Economics, history, sociology
     _____ G.   Journalism, English

_____ H. Business administration
_____ I. Public administration
_____ J. Other: _____

24. Your present annual salary level:

_____ A. $5,000 or less
_____ B. $5,001 to $7,500
_____ C. $7,501 to $10,000
_____ D. $10,001 to $15,000
_____ E. $15,001 to $17,500
_____ F. $17,501 to $20,000
_____ G. $20,001 to $25,000
_____ H. $25,001 or above

25. Total years of municipal government service:

_____ A. 3 or less
_____ B. 4–5 years
_____ C. 6–7 years
_____ D. 8–9 years
_____ E. 10–11 years
_____ F. 12–13 years
_____ G. 14–15 years
_____ H. over 15 years

26. Were you promoted to your present position from another post in the same municipal government?

_____ A. Yes
_____ B. No

27. Position which you held immediately prior to your present position:

_____ A. Assistant city manager
_____ B. Chief administrative officer
_____ C. Personnel director
_____ D. City engineer
_____ E. Police chief

_____ F.   Line department head
_____ G.   Business executive
_____ H.   City manager, smaller city
_____ I.   City manager, larger city
_____ J.   Other: _____

Thank you very much for your cooperation. Please place questionnaire in the enclosed self-addressed envelope and mail!

Appendix C

A Typological Note

C–1. City Managers
and Policy Role Orientations

The major policy role orientations (Political Leader, Political Executive, Administrative Director, and Administrative Technician) are based on manager responses to nine closed questions. City managers were asked as follows:

Now ever since the council-manager plan was first adopted, there has been much disagreement over what a city manager should or should not do. Here are nine questions on the job of being a city manager. Read each question and then decide which one of the four answers most closely describes how you feel—do you strongly agree, tend to agree, tend to disagree, or strongly disagree? Circle the answer you select!

1. A CITY MANAGER SHOULD ADVOCATE MAJOR CHANGES IN CITY POLICIES.
   A–strongly agree   B–tend to agree
   C–tend to disagree   D–strongly disagree

2. A CITY MANAGER SHOULD GIVE A HELPING HAND TO GOOD COUNCILMEN WHO ARE COMING UP FOR REELECTION.
   A–strongly agree   B–tend to agree
   C–tend to disagree   D–strongly disagree

3. A CITY MANAGER SHOULD MAINTAIN A NEUTRAL STAND ON ANY ISSUES ON WHICH THE COMMUNITY IS DIVIDED.
A–strongly agree   B–tend to agree
C–tend to disagree   D–strongly disagree

4. A CITY MANAGER SHOULD CONSULT WITH THE COUNCIL BEFORE DRAFTING HIS OWN BUDGET.
A–strongly agree   B–tend to agree
C–tend to disagree   D–strongly disagree

5. A CITY MANAGER SHOULD ASSUME LEADERSHIP IN SHAPING MUNICIPAL POLICIES.
A–strongly agree   B–tend to agree
C–tend to disagree   D–strongly disagree

6. A CITY MANAGER SHOULD ENCOURAGE PEOPLE WHOM HE RESPECTS TO RUN FOR THE CITY COUNCIL.
A–strongly agree   B–tend to agree
C–tend to disagree   D–strongly disagree

7. A CITY MANAGER SHOULD ACT AS AN ADMINISTRATOR AND LEAVE POLICY MATTERS TO THE COUNCIL.
A–strongly agree   B–tend to agree
C–tend to disagree   D–strongly disagree

8. A CITY MANAGER SHOULD ADVOCATE POLICIES TO WHICH IMPORTANT PARTS OF THE COMMUNITY MAY BE HOSTILE.
A–strongly agree   B–tend to agree
C–tend to disagree   D–strongly disagree

9. A CITY MANAGER SHOULD WORK THROUGH THE MOST POWERFUL MEMBERS OF THE COMMUNITY TO ACHIEVE POLICY GOALS.
A–strongly agree   B–tend to agree
C–tend to disagree   D–strongly disagree

Comments: _____

_____

The responses to each question were scored according to +3 for strongly agree, +1 for tend to agree, —1 for tend to disagree, and —3 for strongly disagree. And then the response scores for each manager were summed over the nine questions. (It should be noted that the scores for items 3, 4, and 7 were reversed in order to make the results consistent with the direction of the other six items.) The summed scores identify the relative direction and intensity of the commitment by Bay Area managers to participate in and influence the policy process:

Summed Scores for Bay Area Managers (N = 58)

+	+	−	−
+27	+13—1	−1—4	−15—2
26	12—1	2	16
25	11—3	3—2	17
24	10	4	18
23	9—5	5—3	19
22	8	6	20
21	7—9	7—2	23
20	6—1	8—1	22
19	5—3	9—1	23
18	4	10	24
17—2	3—7	11	25
16	2	12—1	26
15—5	1—5	13	27
14	0	14	

From these summed scores, city managers were classified as having one of four policy role orientations: Political Leader, +11 and above; Political Executive, +4 to +10; Administrative Director, −2 to +3; and Administrative Technician, −3 and below. These cutoff points were assigned after a careful inspection of the results in search of role patterns and policy standards and in order to divide the managers, for purposes of analysis, into more or less equal groups. Though the policy orientations are thus empirical constructs, largely determined by the actual responses of Bay Area managers, they were derived from questions and procedures applicable to any sample of city managers. Further, it is assumed that these policy orientations provide reliable and valid measures of policy role differences no matter what the sample of city managers.

C–2. City Councilmen
and Policy Orientations for Manager

The rules and procedures for typing councilmanic views of the manager are, with several minor changes, the same as those for typing the policy orientations of city managers. City councilmen were asked ten closed questions:

Here are some statements which reflect different viewpoints about the job of city manager or top administrator. We would like to know how you feel about these viewpoints. Would you please check just how much you generally agree or disagree with each. The city manager or other top administrator should:

1. maintain a neutral stand on any issues which divide the community.
    - _____ Agree
    - _____ Tend to agree
    - _____ Tend to disagree
    - _____ Disagree
2. consult with the Council before drafting his own budget proposal.
    - _____ Agree
    - _____ Tend to agree
    - _____ Tend to disagree
    - _____ Disagree
3. assume leadership in shaping municipal policies.
    - _____ Agree
    - _____ Tend to agree
    - _____ Tend to disagree
    - _____ Disagree
4. act as an administrator and leave policy matters to the Council.
    - _____ Agree
    - _____ Tend to agree
    - _____ Tend to disagree
    - _____ Disagree
5. advocate policies even if important parts of the community seem hostile to them.

_____ Agree
_____ Tend to agree
_____ Tend to disagree
_____ Disagree

6. give a helping hand to good councilmen who are coming up for reelection.

_____ Agree
_____ Tend to agree
_____ Tend to disagree
_____ Disagree

7. advocate major changes in city policies if necessary.

_____ Agree
_____ Tend to agree
_____ Tend to disagree
_____ Disagree

8. encourage people whom he respects to run for the Council.

_____ Agree
_____ Tend to agree
_____ Tend to disagree
_____ Disagree

9. work through the most powerful members of the community to achieve his policy goals.

_____ Agree
_____ Tend to agree
_____ Tend to disagree
_____ Disagree

10. work informally with councilmen to prepare important policy proposals.

_____ Agree
_____ Tend to agree
_____ Tend to disagree
_____ Disagree

As with city managers, the responses to each question were scored according to $+3$ for agree, $+1$ for tend to agree, -1 for tend to disagree, and -3 for disagree. And then the response scores for each councilman were summed over the ten questions. (Again, to make the results consistent with the direction of the other items, the scores for items 1, 2, and 4 were reversed.) The summed scores identify the extent to which city councilmen feel the city manager should be a policy partisan:

Summed Scores for Bay Area Councilmen (N = 351)

+	+	−	−
+30	+12—5	−1—1	−16—10
29	11	2—26	17—1
28	10—4	3—3	18—12
27	9—1	4—23	19—1
26	8—12	5—2	20—6
25	7—1	6—26	21
24—1	6—16	7—2	22—4
23	5	8—26	23—1
22	4—19	9	24—12
21	3—6	10—22	25
20	2—27	11	26—2
19—1	1—2	12—31	27—1
18—1	0—16	13—1	28
17		14—20	29
16		15	30—3
15—1			
14—1			
13—1			

Using almost the same cutoff points as for city managers, councilmen were classified as having one of five views of the policy role of the city manager: Political Leader, +11 and above; Political Executive, +4 to +10; Administrative Director, —3 to +3; Administrative Technician, —4 to —10; and Administrative Assistant, —11 and below. Three noteworthy differences exist, however, between these measures of policy role orientations and those for city managers. The most obvious difference is a fifth type, Administrative Assistant. The purpose here was to recognize the very strong objections many councilmen have to any participation and influence by the city manager in the policy process.

The other two differences work to bias councilmanic responses in favor of a "broader" definition of the city manager's policy role. First, city councilmen are asked one more question (item 10) and one question (item 7) is significantly reworked. Both these questions are worded in such a manner as to solicit a positive response from city councilmen. For example, it would seem difficult not to agree (though 179 councilmen dissent) that a city manager should "advocate major changes in city policies if necessary." And, second, the closed choices of city councilmen—agree, tend to agree, tend to disagree, and disagree—should encourage more +3 responses than those choices open to city managers—strongly agree, tend to agree, tend to disagree, and strongly disagree. Nevertheless, despite these differences, councilmen and manager scores on similar closed questions provide a useful format for identifying, comparing, and interpreting major variations in city councilmen's views of the policy role of the city manager.

Appendix D

The Research Project and the Data

This Appendix provides a brief *description* of the *context* for the analyses and interpretations reported in this and the other monographs of *The Urban Governors* series. These analyses and interpretations are grounded in or inspired by data collected at a specific "point" in time—actually over a period of some eighteen months, from January 1966 to June 1967—in a particular region of the United States. The data are "representative," therefore, in only a very limited sense. Although none of the writers of each monograph would claim greater universality for his interpretations than the data warrant, the temptation on a reader's part to forget or ignore the limitations of a clearly bounded space-time manifold is always present. The reader is entitled, therefore, to information about the setting of each study, if only for comparison with settings which are more familiar to him and which serve as his own frames of reference.

Needless to say, we cannot describe here the San Francisco Bay metropolitan region, its cities and its people, in their full richness and diversity. Clearly, only certain aspects of the environment are relevant, and this relevance must be determined by the objectives of the particular research project in which we were engaged. Before presenting the relevant context, therefore, the research project itself will be described in brief outline.

The City Council Research Project

As mentioned already in the Preface, the Project was a research and training program with as many as twelve participants working together at one time. Because the Project was intended, from the beginning, to maximize the independent research creativity of each participant, the research design had to be sufficiently flexible to permit the collection of data which would satisfy each Project member's research concerns. The monographs in this series reflect the heterogeneity of the research interests which found their way into the Project. At the same time, each researcher was necessarily limited by the Project's overall objective, which was, throughout, to gather data which would shed light on the city council as a small political decision-making group.

Our interest in the city council as a decision-making group stemmed from prior research on governance through democratic legislative processes. Political scientists have been traditionally concerned with the variety of "influences," external to the legislative body as well as internal, that shape both the legislative process and the legislative product. It was an assumption of the research that these influences could be studied more intensively in the case of small bodies than in the case of larger ones, like state legislatures or Congress, that already have been widely investigated. In particular, it was assumed that a decision-making body is both the sum of its parts and greater than the sum of its parts. Therefore, both the council as a collective unit and the councilman as an individual unit could be selected for the purposes of analysis. In the major book of this series, by Heinz Eulau and Kenneth Prewitt, the council as such serves as the unit of analysis. In the accompanying monographs, individual councilmen primarily serve as the units.

Convenience apart, the choice of the universe to be studied was dictated by the research objective. On the one hand, we needed a sufficiently large number of decision-making groups to permit systematic, quantitative, and genuinely comparative analyses at the group level. On the other hand, we needed a universe in which "influences" on the individual decision maker and the decision-making group could be studied in a relatively uniform context.

In particular, we sought a universe which provided a basic environmental, political, and legal uniformity against which city-by-city differences could be appraised. We therefore decided on a single metropolitan region in a single state in which we could assume certain constants to be present—such as *relative* economic growth, similar institutional arrangements and political patterns, identical state statutory requirements, and so on.

The price paid for this research design should be obvious. The San Francisco Bay metropolitan region is quite unlike any other metropolitan region, including even the Los Angeles metropolitan area, and it differs significantly from the Chicago, Boston, or New York metropolitan complexes. Undoubtedly, metropolitan regions, despite internal differences, can be compared as ecological units in their own right. But as our units of analysis are individual or collective decision makers in the cities of a particular, and in many respects internally unique region, the parameters imposed on our data by the choice of the San Francisco Bay metropolitan area recommend the greatest caution in extending, whether by analogy or inference, our findings to councils or councilmen in other metropolitan regions of other states.

All of this is not to say that particular analyses enlightened by theoretical concerns of a general nature cannot be absorbed into the growing body of political science knowledge. The City Council Research Project consciously built on previous research in other settings, seeking to identify and measure influences that have an impact on legislative processes and legislative products. The effect of the role orientations of councilmen with regard to their constituents, interest groups, or administrative officials may be compared with the effect of parallel orientations in larger legislative bodies. Their socialization and recruitment experiences, their differing styles of representational behavior, or their political strategies are probably influences not unlike those found elsewhere. Similarly, the relationships among individuals in a small group and the norms guiding their conduct may be compared with equivalent patterns in larger legislative bodies. Perceptions of the wider metropolitan environment and its problems, on one hand, and of the city environment and its problems, on the other hand, and how these perceptions affect council behavior and outputs are of general theoretical interest. In terms of the developing theory of legislative behavior and processes, therefore, the data collected by the Project and utilized in the monographs of this series have an import that transcends the boundaries of the particular metropolitan region in which they were collected.

The Research Context

San Francisco and its neighboring eight counties have experienced an extraordinary population growth rate since the end of World War II. Many of the wartime production workers and military personnel who traveled to or through this region decided to settle here permanently in the postwar years; they and thousands of others were attracted by moderate climate year around, several outstanding universities, closeness to the Pacific Ocean and its related harbors, headquarters for hundreds of West Coast branches of national firms and, of course, the delightful charm of San Francisco itself. Other resources and assets exist in abundance: inviting ski resorts and redwood parks are within short driving distance; hundreds of miles of ocean lie to the immediate west; mile after mile of grape vineyards landscape the nearby Livermore and Napa valleys. All of these, linked by the vast San Francisco Bay and its famous bridges, make this one of the nation's most distinctive and popular metropolitan regions.

Larger than the state of Connecticut and almost as large as New Jersey and Massachusetts combined, this nine-county region now houses four million people; about six million more are expected by 1980. At the time of the study, ninety cities and at least five hundred special districts served its residents.

As has been pointed out already, no claim can be made that the San Francisco Bay region is typical of other metropolitan areas; indeed, it differs considerably on a number of indicators. Unlike most of the other sizable metropolitan regions, the Bay region has experienced its major sustained population boom in the 1950s and 1960s. This metropolitan area is also atypical in that it has not one major central city but three—namely San Francisco, Oakland, and San Jose. And while San Francisco continues to be the "hub" and the region's dominant city, Oakland and San Jose are rival economic and civic centers. San Jose, moreover, anticipates that its population will triple to nearly a million people in the next twenty years. Of additional interest is the fact that this region has pioneered in the creation of one of the nation's prototypes of federated urban governmental structures. Its Association of Bay Area Governments, organized in 1961, has won national attention as one of the first metropolitan councils of local governments.

Although in many respects unlike other metropolitan regions, the San Francisco Bay region resembles some in the great diversity among its cities. Omitting San Francisco proper, 1965 city populations ranged from 310 to 385,700. Population densities in 1965 ranged from 71 to 12,262 persons per square mile. The rate of population growth between 1960 and 1965 ranged from zero to 204 percent. Median family incomes ranged from $3,582 to $23,300, and percentage nonwhite from 0.1 to 26.4.

Institutionally, the governments of the cities in the San Francisco Bay region are predominantly of the council-manager or council-administrator form, although some of the very small cities may rely on the chief engineer rather than on a manager or administrator. Cities may be either of the "charter" or "general law" type. Charter cities differ from general law cities in having greater control over election laws, the size of their councils, the pay of municipal officers, and tax rate limitations. General law cities have five councilmen, while charter cities may have more than this number. Among the cities included in the research, the number of councilmen per city ranged from five to thirteen.

All local officials in California, including, of course, those interviewed in the City Council Research Project, are elected under a nonpartisan system. With a few exceptions, councilmen run at large and against the entire field of candidates. In five cities there is a modified district election plan in which candidates stand in a particular district but all voters cast ballots for any candidate. Ten cities elect the mayor separately; in the remaining cities the mayor is either the candidate receiving the highest number of votes or is selected by vote of the council.

Council candidates must have been residents of the community

Map D–1
Bay Area Place Names

N

Cloverdale

Gualala R.

Russian R.

SONOMA

Fort Ross

Healdsburg

Guerneville

Calistoga

Lake Berryessa

NAPA

St. Helena

Sebastopol

Santa Rosa

Bodega Bay

Glen Ellen

Napa R.

Petaluma

Sonoma

Napa

Vacaville

Dixon

Tomales Bay

SOLANO

Fairfield

MARIN

Drakes Bay

San Pablo Bay

Vallejo

Suisun Bay

Rio Vista

Benicia

San Rafael

Bolinas

Port Costa

Martinez

MT. TAMALPAIS

Richmond

Concord

Pittsburg

Antioch

Sausalito

Berkeley

Orinda

CONTRA

Lafayette

Walnut Creek

Brentwood

San Francisco

S.F.

Oakland

Moraga

Alamo

MT. DIABLO

Alameda

Danville

Byron

Daly City

San Francisco Bay

COSTA

S.

San Francisco

San Leandro

Pacifica

Hayward

Livermore

San Mateo

Union City

Pleasanton

Half Moon Bay

SAN

ALAMEDA

Redwood City

Fremont

MATEO

Palo Alto

Pescadero

Santa Clara

San Jose

SANTA

Saratoga

Big Basin

Los Gatos

MT. HAMILTON

San Lorenzo R.

Guadalupe R.

CLARA

SANTA

Morgan Hill

Santa Cruz

CRUZ

Gilroy

0 5 10   20   30

Miles

Monterey Bay

Watsonville

213

for at least one year prior to their election. For the most part they are elected to serve two-year terms, though charter cities may vary this. Only three cities have tenure limitations. The great majority of councilmen receive no compensation for their services or, if any, only a token compensation to cover expenses. For most, the council is a part-time activity.

The powers of the city councilmen may be exercised only as a group; that is, individual councilmen have no power to act alone. The council may meet only at duly convened public meetings and at a place designated by ordinance. Council meetings must be regularly scheduled and held no less than once a month, but when council action is required between regularly scheduled meetings, the statutes allow procedures for calling special meetings. The "Brown Act," passed in 1953 and in effect during the time our interviewing took place, requires all council meetings to be public and publicized, except for executive sessions on personnel matters.

The Data Bases

Five sets of data were generated or systematized by the Project. First, data from the U.S. Census of Population for 1960 and estimates for 1965 served a variety of analytical purposes. Because the data included in the census and its categories are well known, we need not say more about this data set. Specific uses made of census data and the rationale for such uses are explained in each monograph wherever appropriate. All members of the research team were involved in readying the census data for analysis.

Second, data concerning city income, resources, and expenditures were available in the State Controller's *Annual Report of Financial Transactions Concerning Cities of California.* These reports include breakdowns which are suitable for comparative analysis of Bay region cities for the year 1958–59 through 1965–66. How the measures derived from this data set were handled is described in appropriate places of the monograph series where the data are used. Robert Eyestone was largely responsible for preparing this data set.

Third, local election data over a ten-year period, 1956 through 1966, were collected by Gordon Black, with the collaboration of Willis D. Hawley at the Institute of Governmental Studies, University of California, Berkeley. These data were obtained directly from the various cities, and they include the voting returns for each of five elections in each city, the registration figures for the city at each election period, and a variety of facts about individual candidates. These facts include incumbency, partisan affiliation, length of time in office, and the manner in which the incumbents gained office, whether by appointment or by election. A number of measures were constructed from these data, including measures of competition, partisan composition, voluntary retirement, forced turnover, and so forth. Descriptions of these measures can be found in the monographs which employ them.

Fourth and fifth, the core of the data on which the analyses are based came from interviews with city councilmen or from self-administered questionnaires filled out by councilmen. These two data sets need more detailed exposition.

1. *Interview data.* With the exception of a city incorporated while the field work was under way (Yountville) and the city of San Francisco itself, interviews were sought with 488 city councilmen holding office in all the other eighty-nine cities of the San Francisco Bay area. Although interviews were held with some members of the board of supervisors of the city-county of San Francisco, these interviews are not used in this and the other monographs, owing to the city's unique governmental structure and the highly professionalized nature of its legislative body.

In two of the eighty-nine cities (Millbrae and Emeryville), all councilmen refused to be interviewed. In the remaining eighty-seven cities, 435 incumbent councilmen were interviewed. This constitutes 89 percent of the total population or 91 percent of the councilmen from the eighty-seven cities which cooperated in the study. The interviews were conducted by members of the research team or by professional interviewers. Most of the respondents were interviewed in their homes, places of business, or city hall offices. All of them had been invited to visit the Stanford campus, and a small number accepted the invitation and were interviewed there.

Although the bulk of the interviewing was done between January and April 1966, some councilmen were interviewed as late as June 1967. The interview schedule was an extensive one. It included some 165 major open-end questions and additional probes, ranging over a wide variety of topics. Every effort was made to record verbatim the comments which most councilmen supplied in abundance. The interviews lasted from two to five hours or longer and averaged about three hours. Parts of the interview schedule were pretested as early as 1962 and as late as 1965, with councilmen in the metropolitan region itself and with councilmen in a neighboring county.

The interview data were coded by members of the research team responsible for particular analyses. The coded data were recorded on seventeen machine readable storage cards. They will be made available for secondary analysis on tape in due time, upon completion of all studies in *The Urban Governors* series.

2. *Questionnaire.* In addition to the interview, each respondent was asked to fill out a questionnaire made up of closed questions. These included a set of thirty-five check-list items, two pages of biographical items, and a set of fifty-eight agree-disagree attitude items. The strategy of self-administered questionnaires was dictated by the length of the interview, for, in spite of its length, the data needs of the team members could not be satisfied by the interview instrument alone. The questionnaires were left with each respondent by the interviewer. If at all possible interviewers were instructed to have the questionnaires filled out by the respondent immediately upon completion of the interview, but the length of the interview often did not permit this, and respondents were then asked to return the questionnaires by mail. As a result, there was some loss of potential data because councilmen neglected to return the completed forms. Nevertheless, of the 435 councilmen who were interviewed, 365, or 84 percent, completed the questionnaires. Perhaps the greatest strategic mistake in this procedure was our failure to administer the biographical and demographic background items as part of the interview.

The Sample: A Brief Profile

Although individual demographic data for all 435 councilmen who were interviewed are not available, our sample of 365 for which the data are at hand is probably representative. We shall present, therefore, a brief profile of these respondents.

On the average, San Francisco Bay region councilmen are well educated and have comfortable incomes (see Figure D–1). They are engaged in either business or professional activities. Table D–1 shows the principal lines of work of those council members who are not retired or housewives.

Table D–1

Principal Employment of City Councilmen
(Of Employed Councilmen) (N = 351)

Manufacturing, Utilities	22%
Banking, Insurance, Accountancy	21
Business, Commerce, Real Estate	13
Lawyer	10
Construction, Trucking	16
Civil Service, Public Administration	14
Agriculture	4
	100%

Councilmen in the Bay region are predominantly middle-aged, usually coming to the council while in their forties or around fifty years of age. The turnover rate of city councilman positions is relatively high, with only a few members staying in office for more than three or four terms. The data in Figure D–1 show that close to 70 percent of the councilmen came into office for the first time within the previous five years. In open-end conversations with councilmen, many responded that they looked upon the job as a community service, as something that should be rotated among the local activists like themselves.

Fifty-six percent of the Bay region councilmen who are currently employed work in their home community, the community on whose city council they serve. This is not too surprising, for it is customary for local "home town" businessmen and lawyers to

Figure D-1
Background Profile of San Francisco Bay Region
City Councilmen

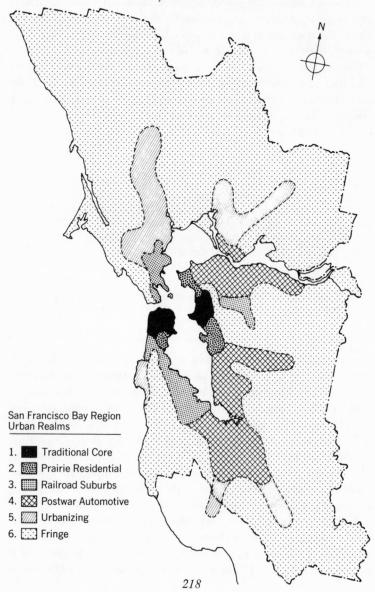

San Francisco Bay Region
Urban Realms

1. Traditional Core
2. Prairie Residential
3. Railroad Suburbs
4. Postwar Automotive
5. Urbanizing
6. Fringe

be involved in community service and civic undertakings, which often constitute the chief recruitment vehicle for the identification of city political leadership. While a majority of the council- men are employed in their local communities, it is instructive to note that most of the councilmen are not natives of their present city or county. Most, however, are California or West Coast na- tives. Approximately a third moved to the Bay region from other parts of the United States, with about a dozen having been born in some other country.

The background profile data also indicate that Republicans outnumber the Democrats by an 11 percent margin in the Bay region's nonpartisan city council posts, although during recent years the party registration rates for the general electorate have favored the Democratic party in approximately a three-to-two ratio. Nine percent of the councilmen identify themselves as Independents.

Index